Careers
for Humanists

Careers
for Humanists

ERNEST R. MAY

*Department of History and
John F. Kennedy School of Government
Harvard University
Cambridge, Massachusetts*

DOROTHY G. BLANEY

*University of the State of New York
State Education Department
Albany, New York*

ACADEMIC PRESS
A Subsidiary of Harcourt Brace Jovanovich, Publishers
New York   London
Paris   San Diego   San Francisco   São Paulo
Sydney   Tokyo   Toronto

ACADEMIC PRESS, INC.
111 Fifth Avenue, New York, New York 10003

United Kingdom Edition published by
ACADEMIC PRESS, INC. (LONDON) LTD.
24/28 Oval Road, London NW1 7DX

Library of Congress Cataloging in Publication Data

May, Ernest R.
    Careers for humanists.

    Includes bibliographical references and index.
    1. Education, Humanistic--United States.
2. College teaching--Vocational guidance--United
States. 3. Vocational guidance--United States.
4. Doctor of philosophy degree. I. Blaney,
Dorothy G. II. Title.
LC1011.M32   001.3'07'1173   81-15000
ISBN 0-12-480620-1   AACR2

PRINTED IN THE UNITED STATES OF AMERICA

81 82 83 84   9 8 7 6 5 4 3 2 1

To the memory of
Allan M. Cartter

2186944

Contents

Preface

Since the mid-1970s, higher education has been a declining industry. It promises to remain so, even if the rest of the economy prospers. Seeing this prospect, many people have expressed concern about implications for basic research. Most of these people focus on the natural or social sciences. We address here implications for the humanities—history and criticism, other types of history, philosophy, and related subjects.

If the nation is in the early stages of a long-swing depression in higher education, what assumptions can realistically be made about numbers of career openings in college teaching for students of literature, historians, and philosophers? How many people will enroll for graduate training in these disciplines? How many of them will complete that training? These are the subjects of Chapters 1 and 2.

Chapter 3 reviews careers other than college teaching followed by people with doctoral training in the humanities. On the basis of questionnaire responses and interviews, we report on how these people have enjoyed their work, how and whether they have found their scholarly training useful, how their lives have compared with those of classmates who became professors, and what they have done avocationally as scholars.

Our final chapter then asks what can be done, and by whom,

to protect and advance humanistic scholarship during a long period in which career openings on college faculties are likely to be scarce or financially unrewarding, or both. At worst, conditions will probably not be as bad as they were in the 1930s—and the humanities flourished in the 1930s. What are the chances that, no matter what the conditions in colleges and graduate schools are, the decades ahead will see rich production of scholarly books and articles? Assuming that neither government agencies nor foundations are likely to add much to what they now invest in the humanities, could they so redirect their spending as to make such an outcome more likely?

To all questions, our answers are at best tentative and suggestive. We offer projections of teaching openings and graduate enrollments. They are projections, not forecasts, for people who foresee futures they do not want can sometimes take steps to make those futures different. The condition of the humanities in America by the end of the twentieth century will be determined by thousands of discrete decisions by professors, university administrators, undergraduates debating whether to go to graduate school, graduate students planning their own careers, foundation officers, government officials, legislators, and others. Our hope is that this book may help some of these people make their decisions more reflectively.

Acknowledgments

We began work on this book in collaboration with Allan M. Cartter of UCLA and Lewis C. Solmon of the Higher Education Research Institute. Cartter died in 1976, but this book and its companion, *Alternative Careers for Humanities Ph.D.'s: Perspectives of Students and Graduates*, by Lewis C. Solmon, Nancy L. Ochsner, and Margo-Lea Hurwicz, both owe a great deal to his inspiration and instruction.

The surveys referred to in our volume and analyzed in detail by Solmon, Ochsner, and Hurwicz were made possible as a result of a generous grant from the Andrew W. Mellon Foundation and a supplementary grant from the Rockefeller Foundation. We are deeply obligated to Nathan M. Pusey, Jack Sawyer, and Claire List of the former and Joel Colton and Lydia Bronte of the latter.

Many people were kind enough to read and comment on drafts of our book. We are grateful to Bernard and Lotte Bailyn, Harvey Brooks, Bruce Collier, Kenneth Deitch, Richard Freeman, Nathan Keyfitz, Robert Klitgard, Charlotte Kuh, Roy Radner, Glenwood Rowse, Theodora Thayer, Maris Vinovskis, and Paul Wing.

1

How Many Can Teach?

Of 150 million adult Americans, not many more than 100,000 qualify as humanists. Anyone claiming the label probably does not deserve it. Few would even style themselves historians or critics or philosophers. Asked what they are, most answer "teacher" or "professor." For, in living memory, history, literature, and philosophy have been seriously studied in the United States chiefly by people teaching in colleges or universities. All but a handful of scholars in these fields are either teachers or students enrolled in doctoral programs.

In 1930 the number of full-time college teachers was approximately 82,000. The number of graduate students was 47,000. These statistics included teachers and graduate students in all academic fields—science, education, and business as well as the humanities. By 1950 the number of teachers had doubled and the number of graduate students had increased sixfold. At the end of the 1970s, the Office of Education's National Center for Education Statistics (NCES) reported full-time college teachers numbering in the neighborhood of 450,000, and graduate students, full-time and part-time, numbering over a million.[1]

---

[1] National Center for Education Statistics, *Digest of Education Statistics* (annual) and *The Condition of Education* (1980).

The number of college teachers in the humanities had not grown at an equivalent rate. Twenty percent of the total in earlier years, they formed smaller proportions later. A survey of department heads conducted in the mid-1970s by the Higher Education Research Institute (HERI) found the number of full-time faculty teaching English, modern languages, history, and philosophy to be about 61,000, which was only 14% of the total full-time college faculty counted contemporaneously by the NCES. (See Table 1.1.) Though no comparable survey has been made since the mid-1970s, the American Historical Association estimates the number of full-time college teachers of history to have fallen from 12,900 in 1975 to 10,875 in 1980 — from 3% of all college teachers to about 2.4%. Opportunities for humanists to earn a living through college teaching appear to be dwindling.

Because of the traditional link between college teaching and scholarship in the humanities, the first question to be asked concerns the number of such opportunities there are likely to be during the next decade or two. To estimate this number is not simple. To estimate openings in particular disciplines is harder still. Associations of engineers have regularly projected shortages and then after a few years had to say red-facedly that in actuality surpluses had developed. As Richard Freeman has explained, forecasts attracted college freshmen and sophomores to engineering and thus created a later glut.[2] Anyone trying to project demand for college teachers has to take warning from this example and also to bear in mind the possible influence of some event not now foreseen. The history of American higher education became very different after October 1957, when the Soviet Union launched its first Sputnik spacecraft and thereby provoked national alarm about the state and prospects of American science and engineering. Some such unexpected event could occur again.

[2] See Richard B. Freeman, *The Overeducated American* (New York: Academic Press, 1976), pp. 112–117, and other works cited there.

Table 1.1
Estimated Full-Time College and University Faculty in English, Modern Languages, History, and Philosophy, 1955–1975[a]

Year	Field				
	English	Modern languages	History	Philosophy	Total
1955	12,100(9.3)	6,600(5.1)	5,000(3.9)	2,100(1.6)	25,800(20)
1960	14,900(9.1)	8,500(5.2)	7,000(4.3)	2,800(1.7)	33,200(20)
1965	22,100(8.8)	13,100(5.3)	10,700(4.3)	4,200(1.7)	50,100(20)
1970	32,400(8.8)	17,300(4.7)	14,000(3.8)	5,500(1.5)	69,200(19)
1975	27,100(6.3)	15,500(3.6)	12,900(3.0)	5,200(1.2)	60,700(14)

Sources: National Education Association, Research Division, *Teacher Supply and Demand in Colleges, Universities, and Junior Colleges*, published annually from 1955 to 1965; R. E. Dunham, Patricia Wright, and Marjorie Chandler, *Teaching Faculty in Universities and Four-Year Colleges* (Washington, D.C.: U.S. Office of Education, 1966); National Center for Education Statistics (NCES), *Teaching and Research Staff by Academic Field in Institutions of Higher Education, Fall 1967* (Washington, D.C., 1968) and *Fall 1968* (Washington, D.C., 1969); unpublished NCES data for 1970; responses from heads of English, French, Spanish, German, history, and philosophy departments to a questionnaire sent to all of them by the Higher Education Research Institute in academic 1975–1976, asking, among other things, for comparative numbers of faculty in 1965, 1970, 1974, and 1975; and information supplied by the Modern Language Association, the American Historical Association, and the American Philosophical Association. Percentages are based on counts or estimates of full-time faculty in NCES, *Digest of Education Statistics* (annual), and *The Condition of Education* (1980).

[a] Percentages of total full-time faculty are given in parentheses.

How Many Can Teach?

Demand for college teachers, however, is not quite the same as demand for engineers. New jobs for engineers can be created by new technology, by shifts in public interest—as from clean air to energy—or by many other changes; however, new jobs for college teachers can develop from one of only three conditions: (*a*) more students; (*b*) fewer students per teacher; and (*c*) replacement needs created by deaths, retirements, and resignations.

Since most of the college-age population has already been born, the pool of potential students is known, and projections can be made of numbers likely to attend college. Extrapolation from historical evidence on student–teacher ratios, turnover rates, and proportions in particular fields can yield projections of numbers of openings for teachers. A review of what such extrapolation would have yielded in the past suggests that the projections deserve to be taken seriously.

It is instructive to consider projections that simple assumptions would have produced in the middle of 1957, with no intimation that Sputnik I would soon go into orbit. As of July 1957, Census Bureau data showed a national birthrate that had been rising on a gradient resembling the takeoff path of a jet plane. Junior high schools and elementary schools were aswarm. The freshmen for the first half of the 1970s, then in cradles and playpens, were even more plentiful. Over the preceding century, moreover, the proportions of youngsters graduating from high school and going on to college had been steadily going up. With a graph of these past trends and a volume of *Vital Statistics,* anyone able to use a slide rule could have projected mid-1970s college enrollments of between 8 and 10 million—the lower figure if the 1920–1956 curve were extrapolated, the higher if only the curve of 1946–1956 were extended. In actuality, enrollments were to total just under 10 million.

To go on to estimate demand for faculty would have involved more guesswork. Although historical data on population and enrollment trends might have been suspect, they were wonderfully precise as compared with data on faculty, for criteria used to distinguish full-timers from part-timers and senior faculty from junior faculty varied from institution to institution and year to year. (Who are considered faculty and who are not, how they are counted and by whom, it should be said, remain unclear.) As of 1957, one could have done no better than to assume that the ratio of faculty, full-time and part-time, to students, also full-time and part-time, would remain around 1:10, as over most of the preceding century. Such an assumption would have yielded a projection that total college faculty by the mid-1970s would be between 800,000 and 1 million. And, in fact, official counts as of 1976 were to put total faculty at around 950,000. (See Table 1.2.)

A projection of full-time faculty would have been equally near the bull's-eye. As of the mid-1950s, more than a third of the total college faculty consisted of teaching assistants and others not filling the category of "faculty, instructor and above." Of those considered faculty, 3 out of 10 were employed part-time. Hence, for practical purposes, full-time faculty represented about 44% of total faculty. On an assumption that this proportion would remain constant, estimated numbers of full-time faculty as of the mid-1970s would have run between 350,000 and 440,000. The actual figure was to be around 430,000. (See Table 1.3.)

By assuming that the proportion of full-time faculty in the humanities would remain constant, at about 20%, one would have forecast an increase from 30,000 to about 80,000. In reality, as already noted, the proportion of faculty in these fields dipped to below 14%, with the resulting 1975 total almost 20,000 below what would have been projected.

Estimates made in 1957 from very crude assumptions and data, without foreknowledge of Sputnik, would thus have been inexact but not wholly detached from reality. What developed in aggregate enrollments, faculty, and even full-time faculty fell well within the range of what would have been projected. A guess as to faculty totals in the humanities would

Table 1.2
Population Aged Eighteen to Twenty-Four Compared with Total Degree-Credit Enrollments and Total Faculty in American Colleges and Universities, 1870–1976

| Year | Population aged 18–24 (millions) | Total degree-credit enrollments | | Total faculty[a] (thousands) | Ratio of faculty to total enroll-ments |
		Number (thousands)	Percentage of popula-tion aged 18–24		
1870	4.7	52	01.1	6	1:9
1880	7.3	116	01.6	12	1:10
1890	8.7	157	01.8	16	1:10
1900	10.3	238	02.3	24	1:10
1910	9.1	264	02.9	36	1:7
1920	12.7	598	04.7	49	1:12
1930	15.3	1101	07.2	82	1:13
1940	16.4	1494	09.1	147	1:10
1950	16.1	2281	14.2	247	1:9
1956	15.0	2918	19.5	299	1:10
1960	16.1	3583	22.2	381	1:9
1966	21.4	5928	27.7	596	1:10
1970	24.7	7920	32.1	674	1:12
1976	28.2	9603	34.1	953	1:10

Sources: U.S. Bureau of the Census, *Historical Statistics of the United States* and *Current Population Reports*, Series P-25; National Center for Education Statistics, *Digest of Education Statistics* (annual) and *Projections of Education Statistics* (annual).
[a] Includes full-time and part-time, junior and senior, faculty.

have been off by around 25%. Still, rehearsal of what could have been predicted just on the basis of the national birthrate lends some force to an assumption that birthrate data provide at least a clue to what we are likely to see during the next 18–20 years.

We know with certainty that after 1960 American women began having fewer babies. Although 1 in 8 became a mother during each year of the 1950s, only 1 in 14 was doing so by the late 1970s. It is children of this later period—all of them

Table 1.3

Total Full-Time, Part-Time, and Full-Time-Equivalent College and University Faculty (Instructor or Above), 1956–1980[a]

Year	Faculty (thousands)		
	Full-time	Part-time	Full-time-equivalent
1956	135(68)	63(32)	156
1958	155(68)	72(32)	179
1960	164(67)	81(33)	191
1962	173(65)	92(35)	204
1964	212(69)	95(31)	244
1966	278(77)	84(23)	306
1968	332(78)	96(22)	364
1970	369(78)	104(22)	404
1972	380(76)	120(24)	420
1974	406(72)	161(28)	460
1976	434(69)	199(31)	500
1978	445(69)	202(31)	512
1980	453(68)	209(32)	523

Sources: National Center for Education Statistics, *Digest of Education Statistics* (annual) and *The Condition of Education* (1980).

[a] Percentages of total faculty are given in parentheses.

already alive—who will pass through adolescence and become eligible to go to college between now and the late 1990s. In the 1970s, the group aged 18–21 provided two-thirds to three-quarters of all full-time college enrollments and almost 75% of full-time-equivalent enrollments.[3] In absolute numbers, native-born youth of this age-group will become almost 25% fewer between 1980 and the mid-1990s. Those between 22 and 24 years of age, who have heretofore made up another 15% of the full-time and full-time-equivalent student population,

[3] U.S. Bureau of the Census, *Current Population Reports,* Series P-20, No. 303 (December 1976). (The standard formula for computing full-time-equivalent enrollments or faculty assumes three part-timers equivalent to one full-timer.)

diminish correspondingly but on a slightly different schedule. The group aged 18–24 thus is at its lowest only a little more than 20% smaller. If Census Bureau projections of the birthrate for the early 1980s are accurate, the two age-groups will be expanding again by the end of the century. The 18- to 21-year-old cohort will be about 90% of what it was earlier; the 18- to 24-year-old cohort will be well over 80% of its early 1980s total. (See Table 1.4.)

A larger percentage could, of course, end up in college. Over the long term, the proportion of Americans obtaining college degrees has been increasing. It is not unimaginable that college education will someday be as nearly universal as high-school education. The American Council on Education has developed and publicized possible strategies for increasing college enrollments during the 1980s. In releases aimed at combatting "too much concentration on decline," the American Federation of Teachers has argued that national attention should go instead to the fact that many millions do *not* have college degrees.[4]

Realistically, however, it has to be recognized that the hopes of professional educators may not come true. The ratio between each year's 18-year-olds and each year's high-school graduates leveled off in the 1970s. The ratio between high-school graduates and first-time enrollments in colleges similarly leveled off. (See Table 1.5.) Since some high-school students will always fail or drop out, and some who do not will always work instead of going to college, it could be that the levels of the 1970s are plateaus and that the proportions of young people completing high school and entering college will never increase.

[4] American Council on Education, *College Enrollment: Testing the Conventional Wisdom against the Facts* (Washington, D.C., 1980); Robert M. Nelsen and Irwin H. Polishook, "Academic Morbidity," American Federation of Teachers Higher Education Papers, *Chronicle of Higher Education*, 21 April 1980, p. 9.

Table 1.4
Native-Born College-Age Population, by Age-Group, 1975–2000

Year	Population (thousands)		Percentage change from 1980	
	18–21	18–24	18–21	18–24
1975	16,337	27,605	− 4	− 6
1980	16,955	29,462	0	0
1985	15,431	27,853	− 9	− 5
1990	14,719	25,148	− 13	− 15
1995	12,915	23,222	− 24	− 21
2000	14,846	24,653	− 12	− 16

Source: U.S. Bureau of the Census, *Current Population Reports,* Series P-25. (Numbers for 1995 and 2000 are Series II projections.)

Also, it is not wholly impossible that these proportions could decrease. Richard Freeman and some other economists have reasoned that the basic college degree has had declining appeal as it has become worth less in income. White males became able to calculate that over a lifetime the interest on money saved while working for 4 years might match any extra earnings resulting from having a B.A. The estimated rate of return on investment in a B.A. fell from 10% in the early 1970s to only 9% by 1980. When preliminary counts showed college enrollments higher than expected in the fall of 1980, the obvious explanation lay in high unemployment rates and other indications of severe economic recession. If that explanation was valid, the increase is bound to be temporary. If economic conditions become worse, many students will not be able to afford school. If they become better, many will go to work instead of going to school.[5]

[5] Richard B. Freeman, "Overinvestment in College Training?," *Journal of Human Resources* (Summer 1975), pp. 287–311, and *The Market for College-Trained Manpower* (Cambridge, Mass.: Harvard University Press, 1975), *passim.* The rate-of-return estimate appears in *Chronicle of Higher Education,* 22 September 1980, p. 2. Explanations of unexpected enrollment increases are cited *ibid.,* 10 November 1980, p. 3 and 11 May 1981, p. 1.

Table 1.5

Eighteen-Year-Olds, High-School Graduates, and First-Time College Enrollments, 1950–1980

Year	18-year-olds (thousands)	High-school graduates		First-time college enrollments		
		Number (thousands)	Percentage of 18-year-olds	Number (thousands)	Percentage of 18-year-olds	Percentage of high-school graduates
1950	2164	1200	55	517	24	43
1952	2058	1197	58	532	26	44
1954	2135	1276	60	625	29	49
1956	2244	1415	63	715	32	51
1958	2307	1506	65	772	33	51
1960	2613	1864	71	923	35	50
1962	2794	1925	69	1031	37	54
1964	2780	2290	82	1225	44	53
1966	3528	2632	75	1566	44	59
1968	3504	2702	75	1908	54	71
1970	3780	2896	76	2080	55	72
1972	3926	3008	75	2171	55	72
1974	4135	3081	74	2393	58	76
1976	4251	3155	75	2377	56	76
1978	4224	3134	74	2422	57	77
1980	4211	3078	73	2580	61	84

Sources: Allan M. Cartter, *Ph.D.'s and the Academic Labor Market* (New York: McGraw-Hill, 1976), Table 4-2; U.S. Bureau of the Census, *Current Population Reports*, Series P-25; National Center for Education Statistics, *Digest of Education Statistics* (annual) and *The Condition of Education* (1980); and American Council on Education, *1980 Fact Book for Academic Administrators* (Washington, D.C., 1980).

To be sure, students from older age-groups could lift college enrollment levels even if proportions of younger people going to college remained constant or declined. The 1960s and 1970s saw an increase in numbers of students over 24. The hopes of the American Council on Education and the American Federation of Teachers depend in large part on an acceleration of this trend. The fact is, however, that most of the older undergraduates were still in their twenties or early thirties. By the mid-1990s, any new students under 35 will be simply late registrants from their particular cohort of 18-year-olds. Although students over 35 make up more than a tenth of all enrollments, fewer than one in five are full-time students. Since it takes several part-time students to equal one full-timer in terms of demand for faculty, the impact of this older group on prospective numbers of teaching jobs is comparatively small. (See Table 1.6.) For practical purposes, therefore, projections of the student population can be framed on the basis of estimates of the 18- to 24-year-old population and of the proportion of that population likely to enroll in college.[6]

Even if higher education has declining monetary return, the proportion of young Americans going to college probably will not diminish. The worst likely future is one in which conditions remain much like those of the late 1970s. First-year enrollments would then continue to approximate 60% of each year's 18-year-olds; total enrollments, full-time and part-time, would represent about 40% of the population 18–24; and full-time students would form about three-fifths of this total.

If enrollments should increase, they would probably do so gradually rather than abruptly. The proportion of high-school

---

[6] The basic work on enrollment and faculty employment projection is Allan M. Cartter, *Ph.D.'s and the Academic Labor Market* (New York: McGraw-Hill, 1976). A technically more sophisticated review of alternative projections appears in Fred Balderston *et al.*, *Demand and Supply in Higher Education* (New York: McGraw-Hill, 1977). Richard Freeman and David Breneman elaborate methodological problems in *Forecasting the Academic Labor Market*, National Board on Graduate Education Technical Report No. 2 (1974).

Table 1.6
College Enrollments: Total, Full-Time, and Full-Time-Equivalent, 1970–1980

Year	Number (thousands)	Percentage (by age-group)			
		Under 21	22–24	25–34	35 and over
		Total enrollments[a]			
1970	8,649	59	16	18	7
1971	9,025	57	16	19	8
1972	9,298	56	16	19	9
1973	9,694	54	16	20	9
1974	10,322	51	16	22	10
1975	11,291	51	16	22	11
1976	11,121	50	17	22	11
1977	11,415	49	16	24	12
1978	11,392	48	17	22	13
1979	11,700	49	16	24	12
1980	12,087	42	14	27	16
		Full-time enrollments			
1970	5,865	75	15	9	1
1971	6,132	74	15	10	1
1972	6,131	73	15	10	2
1973	6,257	71	16	10	3
1974	6,442	69	15	12	3
1975	6,923	69	15	12	3
1976	6,803	68	17	12	3
1977	6,896	67	16	14	3
1978	6,771	66	17	13	4
1979	6,882	65	17	14	4
1980	7,229	64	17	15	4
		Full-time-equivalent enrollments			
1970	6,793	68	15	13	4
1971	7,096	66	15	14	5
1972	7,187	65	15	14	5
1973	7,403	64	16	15	5
1974	7,735	61	15	17	6
1975	8,379	60	16	17	6
1976	8,242	60	17	17	6

(*continued*)

Careers for Humanists

Table 1.6
(continued)

Year	Number (thousands)	Percentage (by age-group)			
		Under 21	22–24	25–34	35 and over
1977	8,402	59	16	19	7
1978	8,311	58	17	18	7
1979	8,488	58	16	19	7
1980	8,848	57	15	20	8

Sources: For enrollment numbers, American Council on Education, *1980 Fact Book for Academic Administrators* (Washington, D.C., 1980), and National Center for Education Statistics, unpublished and preliminary data; for percentages of each age-group enrolled in college, U.S. Bureau of the Census, *Current Population Reports,* Series P-20.

[a] Includes nondegree-credit enrollments.

graduates could go up. So could the rate at which high-school graduates go on to college. Numbers of new students in their late thirties or older could increase. All of these developments could occur simultaneously. But only an extraordinary and unprecedented surge along all these lines could keep numbers of college students at or even near the levels of the late 1970s.

If, with all else remaining the same, the number of high-school graduates should approximate 90% of the year's 18-year-olds, or if the number of first-time college enrollments should approximate 90% of the year's high-school graduates, the proportion of the 18- to 24-year-old population in college would increase by about 10%—from 40% to 44%. The actual increment would probably be smaller, for it would almost surely include larger numbers of people unwilling or unable to stay in school for more than a year or two. Table 1.7 indicates what total and full-time-equivalent enrollments might be if both of these rates should climb or if, for a combination of reasons, the next 20 years should see the college population actually increase to approximate 50% instead of 40% of the

Table 1.7

Projections of Total Enrollments and Full-Time-Equivalent Enrollments in American Colleges and Universities, 1981–2000[a]

	Total enrollments (millions)		FTE enrollments[b] (millions)	
Year	Low	High	Low	High
1981	11.8 (98)	11.9 (99)	8.8 (99)	8.9 (101)
1982	11.7 (97)	12.0 (99)	8.7 (98)	8.9 (101)
1983	11.6 (96)	12.0 (100)	8.6 (97)	8.9 (100)
1984	11.4 (94)	12.0 (99)	8.4 (94)	8.8 (99)
1985	11.1 (92)	11.8 (98)	8.1 (92)	8.6 (97)
1986	10.8 (90)	11.6 (96)	7.9 (89)	8.4 (95)
1987	10.6 (88)	11.5 (95)	7.6 (86)	8.3 (94)
1988	10.4 (86)	11.4 (95)	7.4 (84)	8.2 (92)
1989	10.3 (85)	11.4 (94)	7.3 (83)	8.1 (92)
1990	10.1 (83)	11.3 (94)	7.1 (81)	8.0 (91)
1991	9.9 (82)	11.2 (93)	7.0 (79)	7.9 (89)
1992	9.7 (80)	11.2 (92)	6.8 (77)	7.8 (88)
1993	9.6 (79)	11.1 (92)	6.7 (75)	7.8 (88)
1994	9.4 (78)	11.1 (92)	6.5 (74)	7.7 (87)
1995	9.3 (77)	11.0 (91)	6.4 (72)	7.6 (86)
1996	9.1 (76)	11.0 (91)	6.3 (71)	7.5 (85)
1997	9.2 (76)	11.1 (92)	6.2 (70)	7.6 (86)
1998	9.3 (77)	11.4 (95)	6.3 (71)	7.8 (88)
1999	9.6 (79)	11.9 (98)	6.4 (73)	8.1 (91)
2000	9.9 (82)	12.3 (102)	6.6 (74)	8.3 (94)

[a] Index values in parentheses: 1980 = 100.
[b] FTE = full-time-equivalent.

population 18 to 24, with three-quarters of the additional students enrolled full-time.

As is apparent, the figures yielded even by this highly optimistic assumption fall far short of satisfying the hopes expressed by educators' organizations. Enrollments still have to be reckoned as dropping significantly below levels of the late 1970s. On the less optimistic assumption that conditions of the late 1970s persist, with the proportion of full-time students dwindling by about a quarter of a percent a year, total enrollments follow the downward trend of the census projections, and full-time-equivalent enrollments fall by as much as

30% (Table 1.7). Yet these numbers probably embrace the boundaries of reality. What seems almost surely in prospect is a long period in which college enrollments are not increasing and may well be decreasing.

If student–faculty ratios should meanwhile remain constant or possibly even worsen, it would follow that employment opportunities in college teaching would fall sharply. Allan Cartter characterized professors as producer goods. Like gem-cutting machines, they create items for consumption. Since each grinds slowly and finely, more have to be added to meet increases in demand, but each lasts a long time. When demand levels off or diminishes, the call for new ones disappears. When enrollments go down, the need for new professors becomes nonexistent. The only new openings stem from resignations, deaths, and retirements, and not all these openings are filled, for some institutions simply reduce staff.

If current ratios were to persist, total numbers of faculty would follow the index numbers in Table 1.7. They would fall either gradually or precipitately. Only in the worst circumstances would the year-to-year drop be so great as to exceed the ordinary rate of attrition due to resignations, deaths, and retirements—a rate that Cartter calculated as averaging 2% a year. Hence, there would usually be some new openings. The totals, however, would be very far from those of the 1960s and 1970s.

Between 1955 and 1980, demand for new full-time faculty averaged over 27,000 a year. Even with the relative decline in openings in the humanities, the demand for teachers of English, modern languages, history, and philosophy ran over 5000 a year. For a time in the middle of the 1960s, new openings for full-time faculty exceeded the total number of new openings for teachers because institutions were upgrading their staff as well as enlarging it. In the humanities, the number of new posts for full-time faculty averaged for a time over 6500 a year. (See Table 1.8.)

Table 1.9 displays how the previous low and high enrollment projections translate themselves into openings for college

Table 1.8
Openings for New Faculty (Instructor or Above) in All Fields and in the Humanities, 1956–1980 (thousands)

| | All faculty | | | | | | Full-time faculty only | | | | | |
| | | Humanities | | | | | | Humanities | | | | |
Year	All fields	English	Modern languages	His- tory	Philos- ophy	Total	All fields	English	Modern languages	His- tory	Philos- ophy	Total
1956	11.8	1.1	.6	.5	.2	2.4	7.6	.7	.4	.3	.1	1.5
1957	23.0	2.1	1.2	.9	.4	4.6	15.7	1.5	.8	.6	.3	3.2
1958	14.3	1.3	.7	.6	.2	2.9	10.0	.9	.5	.4	.2	2.0
1959	15.5	1.4	.8	.6	.3	3.1	9.0	.8	.5	.4	.1	1.8
1960	2.8	.3	.1	.1	.05	.6	(3.8)ᵃ	(.4)	(.2)	(.2)	(.1)	(.8)
1961	16.7	1.5	.9	.7	.3	3.3	11.1	1.0	.6	.5	.2	2.1
1962	22.0	2.0	1.1	.9	.4	4.4	14.2	1.3	.7	.6	.2	2.7
1963	21.3	1.9	1.1	.9	.4	4.3	14.5	1.3	.8	.6	.2	2.7
1964	31.6	2.9	1.6	1.4	.5	6.3	31.7	2.9	1.7	1.4	.5	6.0
1965	39.1	3.5	2.0	1.7	.7	7.8	40.2	3.6	2.1	1.7	.7	7.6
1966	28.8	2.5	1.5	1.2	.5	5.7	35.0	3.1	1.8	1.5	.6	6.6

1967	35.2	3.1	1.9	1.5	.6	7.0	26.6	2.3	1.4	1.1	.4	5.0
1968	45.8	4.0	2.4	1.9	.8	9.1	39.0	3.4	2.0	1.7	.7	7.4
1969	30.6	2.7	1.6	1.3	.5	6.1	24.6	2.2	1.3	1.0	.4	4.6
1970	33.0	2.9	1.7	1.4	.5	6.5	26.0	2.3	1.3	1.1	.4	4.9
1971	27.5	2.4	1.3	1.0	.4	5.2	17.4	1.5	.8	.7	.3	3.1
1972	17.8	1.5	.8	.7	.3	3.3	8.6	.7	.4	.3	.1	1.5
1973	37.0	3.1	1.7	1.4	.5	6.8	16.6	1.4	.8	.6	.2	2.9
1974	50.5	4.3	2.3	1.9	.7	9.2	24.8	2.1	1.1	.9	.4	4.3
1975	72.3	6.0	3.3	2.6	1.0	13.0	42.1	3.5	1.9	1.5	.6	7.2
1976	17.6	1.1	.7	.5	.2	2.5	2.8	.2	.1	.1	.03	.4
1977	29.7	1.9	1.2	.9	.4	4.2	21.7	1.4	.9	.7	.3	2.8
1978	10.0	.6	.4	.3	.1	1.4	6.9	.4	.3	.2	.1	.9
1979	24.9	1.6	1.0	.7	.3	3.5	14.9	.9	.6	.4	.2	1.9
1980	17.2	1.1	.7	.5	.2	2.4	11.0	.7	.4	.3	.1	1.4
Average	27.0	2.3	1.3	1.0	.4	5.0	18.7	1.6	.9	.7	.3	3.4

Note: Calculations are based on the assumption that demand in any given year included all new faculty actually employed and replacements for 2% of the previous year's faculty. Proportions for fields in the humanities are taken from Table 1.1.

[a] Numbers in parentheses indicate negative values.

Table 1.9

Unadjusted Projections of Total and Total Full-Time College and University Faculty and Demand for New Faculty (Instructor or Above) in All Fields and in the Humanities, 1981–2000 (thousands)[a]

Year	Total faculty				Full-time faculty only			
			New openings				New openings	
	Low	High	All fields	Major humanities	Low	High	All fields	Major humanities
1981	649	657	(.7)–6.5[b]	(.1)–.9	440	445	(3.9)–1.1	(.5)–.2
1982	645	661	9.0–17.1	1.3–2.4	436	446	4.8–9.9	.7–1.4
1983	638	662	5.9–13.2	.8–1.8	428	443	.7–5.9	.1–.8
1984	626	657	.8–8.2	.1–1.1	417	438	(2.4)–3.9	(.3)–.5
1985	612	650	(1.5)–6.1	(.2)–.8	406	431	(2.7)–1.8	(.4)–.3
1986	595	640	(4.8)–3.0	(.7)–.4	393	421	(4.9)–(1.4)	(.7)–(.2)
1987	581	632	(2.1)–4.8	(.3)–.7	381	414	(4.1)–1.4	(.6)–.2
1988	571	628	1.6–8.6	.2–1.2	372	409	(1.4)–3.3	(.2)–.4
1989	563	627	3.4–11.6	.5–1.6	365	406	.4–5.2	.1–.7
1990	553	622	1.3–7.5	.2–1.0	356	401	(1.7)–3.1	(.2)–.4
1991	543	617	1.1–7.4	.2–1.0	348	396	(.9)–3.0	(.1)–.4
1992	533	613	.9–8.3	.1–1.2	340	391	(1.0)–2.9	(.1)–.4
1993	527	612	4.7–11.3	.7–1.6	334	389	.8–5.8	.1–.8
1994	519	609	2.5–9.2	.4–1.3	327	385	(.3)–3.8	(.04)–.5
1995	510	606	1.4–9.2	.2–1.3	320	381	(.5)–3.7	(.1)–.5
1996	502	603	2.2–9.1	.3–1.3	313	377	(.6)–3.6	(.1)–.5
1997	504	611	12.0–20.1	1.7–2.8	312	380	5.3–10.5	.7–1.4
1998	513	628	19.1–29.2	2.7–4.1	315	389	9.2–16.6	1.3–2.3
1999	527	653	24.3–37.6	3.4–5.3	322	403	13.3–21.8	1.9–3.1
2000	542	677	25.5–37.1	3.6–5.2	329	416	13.4–21.1	1.9–3.0
Average			5.3–13.3	.8–1.9			1.2–6.4	.2–.9

[a] Figures based on low and high enrollment projections from Table 1.7, assuming constant ratios of 1:18.2 for total faculty to total enrollments and 1:20 for full-time faculty to full-time-equivalent enrollments.

[b] Numbers in parentheses indicate negative values.

teachers if teacher–student ratios and proportions of teachers in the humanities remain roughly the same as at the end of the 1970s. Even with the most optimistic estimates concerning enrollments, total faculty numbers shrink. Numbers of full-time faculty go down even farther. At best, new openings do not come near levels of the past two decades until the very last years of the century. For most of the 1980s and 1990s, the highest projectable annual demand for new faculty in all fields is only one-quarter to one-third the average for the quarter-century ending in 1980. Total projectable openings for full-time faculty in the humanities seldom exceed a few hundred a year.

If these projections were to prove realistic, prudent planning would anticipate that, until the very end of the 1990s, average annual full-time career openings in English would be 70–80, those in either modern languages or history 40–50, and those in philosophy fewer than 20. Even with enrollments in the high range of reasonable projections, the numbers for English would not get much above 200; those for modern languages and history would hover around 100 each; and those for philosophy would be between 40 and 50. And these would be in all types of colleges, 2-year as well as 4-year, and would not necessarily be filled by Ph.D.'s.

In fact, such numbers are probably unrealistically low. In addition to being based on straight-line projections of enrollments, they assume that student–faculty ratios and proportions of faculty in each discipline remain constant. It is more than likely that at least one of these conditions, perhaps both of them, will change.

Some obvious forces should work toward having each teacher teach more students and hence toward there being even fewer job openings. When prices and wages go up in the economy as a whole, costs in colleges and universities go up at an even faster rate; most of what is spent falls in sectors most sensitive to inflation. Historically, services, fuel, and food lead price advances, whereas producer durables and consumer durables trail, and colleges and universities spend more for the former than for the latter—more for janitors, heat, and dormitory meals than for machine tools or even slide projectors. Even if inflation is curbed, the effects of earlier steep increases in college and university budgets and in fees and tuition charges will surely continue to generate demands from administrators and trustees for cost reductions most easily measured in the apparent index of productivity—the student–faculty ratio. Academic departments should find it harder and harder to appoint or replace faculty members who teach esoteric specialties or even to hold on to faculty members who do not attract large enrollments.

At the same time, however, other forces should work in a contrary direction. Many departments will object to offering only subjects that happen currently to be popular among students. In institutions where faculty are strong or there are influential alumni with fond memories of courses on, for example, the Arthurian legend or *Don Quixote* or ancient China, such objections will not be ignored. On broader fronts, faculty assemblies and professors' unions are certain to oppose the phasing out of particular job openings or any general alterations in work rules.

More important still, a decline in enrollments would occur unevenly across the spectrum of institutions of higher education. While many colleges and universities accept anyone able to pay their fees, others turn away students. Of institutions listed in annual issues of the College Entrance Examination Board's *College Handbook*, approximately one-seventh of enrollments are in schools that report that they reject at least 2 out of every 10 applicants. Another two-sevenths are in schools that say they reject 1–2 out of every 10. (See Table 1.10.) If total enrollments decline, most of the comparatively selective institutions should continue to draw students. Some of these institutions might fail because they price themselves out of the market or sink under overhead costs or lose their legislative constituencies. Still, the majority should keep a student population about the size of their current one.

Table 1.10

Colleges and Universities Grouped according to Admission Selectivity (percentages)

	Institutions				Enrollments				Faculty			
	2-year schools	4-year schools			2-year schools	4-year schools			2-year schools	4-year schools		
		Private	Public	Total		Private	Public	Total		Private	Public	Total
Schools turning away 20% or more	1	12	14	28	—	2	6	8	1	16	14	31
Schools turning away 10–20%	—	7	12	19	—	5	16	21	—	9	12	21
Schools accepting 90% or more	22	4	25	52	31	14	27	72	18	4	24	46

Source: College Handbook, 15th–20th eds. (New York and Princeton, N.J.: College Entrance Examination Board, 1976–1980). Total numbers of institutions averaged 2878, which approximates total numbers as estimated by the National Center for Education Statistics.

Of colleges already accepting almost all applicants, many are likely to lose enrollments. A number will probably close. Some, however, will resist. Some 2-year colleges may upgrade themselves to 4-year colleges with a panoply of preprofessional programs and departmental majors. Since 4-year colleges tend to have fewer students per faculty member, these institutions might employ more teachers.

Even among colleges that have had difficulty filling classrooms during the years of expansion, faculty shrinkage would not necessarily match shrinkage in student numbers. Many such colleges exist for reasons other than simple demand for educational services. Two decades or so from now, there may well be a revived demand for higher education. On the basis of this possibility, civic leaders in small towns and suburbs might keep local colleges operating no matter how few young people attend them. Similar decisions might be made by clergymen and laymen responsible for church-related schools. In some instances colleges may be kept alive by loyal alumni.

In demand for college teachers, the more selective and the less selective institutions could, during a long-swing decline, form different markets, virtually walled off from one another. The more selective group could continue to have more or less constant enrollments and hence constant need for replacement faculty, regardless of what happened in the less selective institutions. In Pennsylvania, for example, West Chester State and Gettysburg College, each of which reports turning away one applicant in three, could still need teachers even if Harrisburg Community College and Waynesburg College, which appear to accept nearly all applicants, run short of students and have to lay off faculty. As labor markets, one sector could be merely sluggish, whereas the other could feel most of the effects of ups and downs in enrollments.

If the enrollment decline were 20% or more, somewhat fewer than one-quarter of colleges and universities would not be affected. If the decline were only 10% or so, as many as half could be in that position. Employing disproportionate numbers of faculty and steadily replacing professors who died or retired, these institutions would have between 4000 and 7000 new career openings every year. On the other hand, people not lucky enough to get jobs in selective schools would find themselves competing for a handful of jobs, many in institutions whose own survival might well be in question. (See Table 1.11.)

Of course, however much total faculty numbers may fall, conditions for teachers of English, modern languages, history, and philosophy could be different from conditions for teachers as a whole. During the decades of expansion, proportions in these fields dropped. In part, this shift can be traced to the growth of 2-year colleges, where teachers in the humanities are less in demand. In still larger part, the shift was due to the abandonment or modification of requirements in English, modern languages, and history. Philosophy, a required subject in only a few schools, suffered less of a falling off. (See Table 1.1.) The possibility that a number of 2-year institutions may upgrade themselves, and indications of a trend toward restoration of requirements, suggest an increase in demand for teachers of language, literature, and history in the 1980s and 1990s.

On the other hand, some forces that worked during the 1960s and 1970s to preserve demand for humanities faculty are likely to have less effect in the future. Undergraduates used to be able to indulge their interest in literature or history by rationalizing their studies as possible preparation for a teaching career. As word has circulated about bleak employment prospects and declining pay for teachers, students have turned to other fields. The Higher Education Research Institute surveys found a decrease in college freshmen planning to major in the humanities, from 22% in 1970 to below 5% in 1980.[7] Although this situation may change, nothing in the occupational outlook is likely to make it do so. Fragmentary

---

[7] A. W. Astin *et al.*, *The American Freshman: National Norms for Fall 1970* (Los Angeles: UCLA Graduate School of Education, 1970), and *Chronicle of Higher Education*, 9 February 1981, p. 7.

Table 1.11

Adjusted Projections of Total and Total Full-Time College and University Faculty and Demand for New Faculty, 1981–2000 (thousands)

Year	Total faculty				Full-time faculty only			
	Number	New openings			Number	New openings		
		Selective schools	Nonselective schools	Total		Selective schools	Nonselective schools	Total
1981	651–658	4.1–6.9	(2.8)–1.1[a]	1.3–8.0	453–454	1.9–3.3	7.0–6.9	8.9–10.1
1982	648–661	4.1–6.9	6.4–9.3	10.5–16.2	451–454	1.9–3.3	5.2–6.2	7.1–9.4
1983	643–661	4.1–6.9	3.4–6.6	7.5–13.5	447–453	1.9–3.3	2.9–3.9	4.8–7.2
1984	634–658	4.1–6.9	(.2)–3.3	3.9–10.2	440–448	1.9–3.3	.2–1.2	2.1–4.5
1985	624–654	4.1–6.9	(1.7)–1.7	2.4–8.6	432–442	1.9–3.3	(1.0)–(.1)	.9–3.2
1986	611–647	4.1–6.9	(4.3)–(.8)	(.2)–6.1	422–435	1.9–3.3	(3.0)–(2.1)	(1.1)–1.2
1987	601–641	4.1–6.9	(2.4)–.8	1.7–7.7	414–428	1.9–3.3	(1.5)–(.7)	.4–2.6
1988	593–638	4.1–6.9	.5–3.1	4.2–10.0	408–424	1.9–3.3	.3–1.2	2.2–4.4
1989	587–638	4.1–6.9	2.2–5.1	6.3–12.0	404–422	1.9–3.3	2.0–2.8	3.9–6.1
1990	579–635	4.1–6.9	(.3)–2.6	3.8–9.5	398–418	1.9–3.3	.1–.9	2.0–4.1
1991	572–631	4.1–6.9	(.1)–2.7	4.0–9.6	392–413	1.9–3.3	.2–1.0	2.1–4.2
1992	564–628	4.1–6.9	(.03)–2.7	4.1–9.6	386–409	1.9–3.3	.3–1.0	2.2–4.3
1993	560–628	4.1–6.9	2.5–5.3	6.6–12.2	383–408	1.9–3.3	2.2–3.0	4.1–6.3
1994	554–626	4.1–6.9	1.2–3.9	5.3–10.8	378–405	1.9–3.3	1.2–1.9	3.1–5.2
1995	547–624	4.1–6.9	.8–3.5	4.9–10.4	373–401	1.9–3.3	1.0–1.6	2.9–4.9
1996	541–622	4.1–6.9	.8–3.4	4.9–10.3	369–398	1.9–3.3	.9–1.6	2.8–4.8
1997	542–627	4.1–6.9	7.8–10.9	11.9–17.8	370–401	1.9–3.3	6.3–7.3	8.2–10.6
1998	549–639	4.1–6.9	13.5–17.2	17.6–24.1	375–408	1.9–3.3	10.7–12.1	12.6–15.4
1999	560–655	4.1–6.9	17.8–22.1	21.9–29.0	383–419	1.9–3.3	14.0–15.8	15.9–19.0
2000	571–671	4.1–6.9	18.0–22.6	22.1–29.5	391–430	1.9–3.3	14.1–16.1	16.0–19.3
Average		4.1–6.9	3.2–6.4	7.2–13.3		1.9–3.3	3.1–4.1	5.0–7.3

[a] Numbers in parentheses indicate negative values.

evidence from a few universities suggests that faculty hiring is more a function of numbers of majors than numbers of course enrollments. Except in English composition and elementary foreign language, the return of requirements could bring larger classes without any added demand for faculty.

If there are fewer graduate students in the humanities, that, too, will have a depressing effect, especially at universities where graduate programs kept proportions of faculty in the humanities high when national trends ran otherwise.

Whatever the trend, there will be some openings for college teachers. To be sure, many young professors were hired during the boom of the 1960s and early 1970s. Fewer than two-fifths of the faculty members given life tenure before 1978 will die or retire before the year 2000; at least in 4-year colleges and universities, more than three-quarters of the Ph.D.'s teaching humanities have such tenure. (See Tables 1.12 and 1.13.) For practical purposes, tenured faculty can be fired only if their schools can prove in court inability to pay their salaries. Even so, their numbers do not seriously constrain possibilities for replacement appointments on college and university faculties. In the worst foreseeable circumstance, they do not tie down more than 40% of all faculty posts in English, modern languages, history, and philosophy. (See Table 1.14.)

The key question, both for students contemplating graduate work and for all people concerned about humanistic scholarship, has to do with numbers of additional people who can hope to acquire tenure—to spend their lives on college faculties. These projections, even if one adopts optimistic assumptions about total faculty numbers and hypothesizes a sharp upward trend in the proportions of professors in the major humanities, are disquieting. Until the last years of the century, they do not approach the levels of the 1960s and 1970s. In fact, the most optimistic estimate of the average number of new openings, full-time and part-time, in 1981–2000, is less than half the average for 1956–1980. That for new full-time openings is about a third the average for the earlier period. (Compare Table 1.15 with Table 1.8).

Table 1.12
Tenured Ph.D. Faculty, Full-Time and Part-Time, in English, Modern Languages, History, and Philosophy as of 1980

Year of Ph.D.	Number	Percentage survival rate	Percentage academically employed	Percentage tenured	Estimated number of tenured faculty as of 1980
1940–1942	1,565	88.3	90.7	78	978
1943–1945	777	90.8	90.7	78	499
1946–1948	1,203	92.8	90.7	78	790
1949–1951	2,302	94.4	90.7	78	1,537
1952–1954	2,818	95.9	90.7	78	1,912
1955–1957	2,794	97.0	90.7	78	1,917
1958–1960	3,087	97.9	90.7	78	2,138
1961–1963	3,614	98.6	90.7	78	2,521
1964–1966	5,341	99.0	90.7	78	3,741
1967–1969	7,754	99.4	89.6	71	4,903
1970–1972	11,140	99.7	87.3	51	4,945
1973–1975	12,286	99.9	84.9	33	3,439
1976–1978	10,324	99.9	79.2	14	1,144
Total	65,005				30,463

Sources: For numbers of Ph.D.'s, National Center for Education Statistics' *Earned Degrees* series; for percentages academically employed and percentages tenured, National Research Council, *Employment of Humanities Ph.D.'s* (Washington, D.C., 1980), Tables 21, 23, and 24; for survival rates, National Center for Health Statistics, *Vital Statistics of the United States*. (Rates applied are those for all persons who could have been 30 years of age as of the date when the Ph.D. was conferred.)

Although the numbers of professors with tenure are not large enough to close off all openings, they are sufficient to stir concern among university and college administrators. A tenured teacher usually costs more than a new hire, and administrators will surely try to keep down the proportion of replacement appointees given long-term appointments. The prospect is thus that, in the best of circumstances, comparatively few critics, historians, or philosophers can expect opportunities to spend their lives in college teaching.

Table 1.13

Projections of Retirements and Deaths among Ph.D. Faculty, Full-Time and Part-Time, in English, Modern Languages, History, and Philosophy, Tenured prior to 1978[a]

Year	Estimated retirements	Estimated deaths of preretirement faculty	Total for year	Percentage of total cohort
1980–1982	978	189	1167	4
1983–1985	492	222	714	6
1986–1988	763	250	1013	10
1989–1991	1460	268	1728	15
1992–1994	1791	282	2073	22
1995–1997	1776	292	2068	31
1998–2000	1963	293	2256	38
2001–2003	2298	277	2575	47
2004–2006	3396	228	3624	58
2007–2009	4433	149	4582	73
2010–2012	4458	68	4526	88
2013–2015	3094	16	3110	98
2016–2018	1029	0	1029	100

[a] Figures are based on Table 1.12, assuming retirement 40 years after receipt of Ph.D. and constant mortality rates for age-groups.

For people interested in doing graduate work, teaching for a few years but not making a career of it, openings are likely to be abundant. In fact, the number of short-term vacancies could be much higher than in the past because the proportion of resignations could greatly increase the turnover rate. At the end of the 1970s, academic pay was increasing at 6% a year, but pay in other occupations was going up at an average of 8% a year.[8] Though rates of increase improved at the end of the 1970s, the American Association of University Professors (AAUP) estimated that, in constant dollars, professors' incomes had fallen 20% during the 1970s.[9] If that trend should

[8] Anne O. Krueger, "The Changing Economic Status of the Profession and the Impact of Inflation," *Academe*, vol. 65 (December 1979), pp. 487–492.

[9] "Regressing into the Eighties: Annual Report on the Economic Status of the Profession," *Academe*, vol. 66 (October 1980), pp. 260–320.

Table 1.14

Potential Openings for New Faculty, Full-Time and Part-Time, in the Humanities, 1980–2000 (thousands)[a]

Year	All faculty[b] (average)	Faculty tenured prior to 1978 (average)	Replacement potential openings (average)
1980–1982	89–95	29	60–66
1983–1985	81–100	29	52–71
1986–1988	72–103	28	44–75
1989–1991	64–108	26	38–82
1992–1994	56–112	24	32–88
1995–1997	50–117	22	28–95
1998–2000	46–129	19	27–110

[a] Figures are based on Tables 1.11 and 1.13, assuming that the proportion of faculty in the humanities could decline or increase by somewhat more than 40% between 1980 and 2000 (i.e., from 14% to either 8% or 20%).

[b] Fields included are English, modern languages, history, and philosophy.

continue, a professor netting the same income as a craftsman in 1980 would by the 1990s be taking home less than three-quarters as much. To be sure, the reported figures are deceptive, for at least four out of five faculty members in 4-year colleges and universities supplement their salaries through summer school or extension teaching or other means.[10] With the total student population shrinking, government agencies more selective and relatively less generous in employing professors as consultants, and publishers less free with contracts and advances, opportunities for outside earnings, however, have also waned. The actual economic condition of professors may therefore be even worse than the AAUP reckons.

In consequence, more college teachers may quit for the sake of higher income in some other line of work; humanities professors may not lag behind professors in other fields, for survey data suggest that they are only a little less interested than

[10] *Chronicle of Higher Education,* 17 November 1980, pp. 1, 8.

teachers in other fields in the size of their paychecks.[11] The standard turnover rate could rise above 2%.

It is even possible to develop a plausible argument that numbers of college teachers will remain as high as in the 1960s and 1970s but their salaries will constantly worsen. The basic assumption would be that, although enrollments might trigger an increase in faculty numbers during periods of expansion, revenues would be a more powerful determinant during any long period of contraction.

Enrollment declines would have immediate impact only on the 15–20% of college and university income that is drawn from tuition and fees. Although the 50% or so that comes from the federal government and state and local governments would be affected, lobbying by college administrators, teachers' unions, alumni groups, and civic leaders would prevent reductions from keeping pace with reductions in enrollments. The 30% of income from gifts, interest or endowment, auxiliary enterprises, and so on would not necessarily be affected. Indeed, it might rise. (A college with a smaller number of students could, for example, have more space to rent out for conventions or exhibitions.)

The decline in college and university revenues might thus proceed at less than half the rate of decline in enrollments. Depending on the extent to which operating costs could be held constant and the extent to which faculty members will accept a decline in real wages, total numbers of faculty could remain relatively high. Even with very low enrollments, there could be as many college teaching jobs by the end of the 1990s as at the beginning of the 1980s, if in the meantime faculty

[11] Asked about factors that would be considered essential or very important in seeking another position, 56.2% of a sample of faculty members in the major humanities cited higher salary. In a sample of other faculty, the comparable percentage was 59.2. Alan E. Bayer, *Teaching Faculty in Academe, 1972–73*, American Council on Education Research Reports, vol. 8, No. 2 (1973), and unpublished analyses of the same data prepared by Bayer for the Higher Education Research Institute.

members would settle for real wages up to 15% below the average of 1980. Alternatively, they could keep the average wage of 1980 but see total numbers of job openings vary.[12] (See Table 1.16.)

Despite evidence that demand for faculty in the 1970s could have been reasonably estimated during the late 1950s, the confidence level for any projection is low. The more disaggregated the projection, the lower that level. Hence no one can say with assurance that the 1980s and 1990s will see a certain number of professorships open up in English or history. On the other hand, it is apparent that the forces at work during those decades could well reduce to relatively small numbers the career openings in college teaching suitable for people whose true vocation is humanistic scholarship.

If there is an increase in enrollments, the teaching jobs opened will be chiefly in 2-year colleges and nonselective

---

[12] The model for enrollment-based projections is $F = E/r$, where F is faculty, E is enrollment, and r is the teacher–student ratio. With ample warrant in historical data, Cartter and others have taken r to be more or less fixed. (In the entire period, 1955–1975, the ratio between faculty and full-time-equivalent enrollments shifted from 1 : 16.97 to 1 : 15.75.) For estimating future faculty numbers and demand for new faculty, $F = E/r$ leads to $F_{t+1} = F + qE/r$, where $q = (E_{t+1} - E)/E$. But it is also true that $F = W/w$, where W is the pool of funds available for wages and w is the average wage. An alternative formula for estimating numbers is $F_{t+1} = F + aW/w$, where $a = nq$, with n representing the percentage of W that is influenced by changes in enrollment. In both cases, demand for new faculty is calculated as $\Delta F = (F_{t+1} - F) + yF$, where y represents the average percentage of resignations, retirements, and deaths for the period in question. It is arguable that, in periods of expansion, $F + qE/r$ is quite satisfactory for arriving at F_{t+1} because n approaches 1. On the other hand, when q becomes persistently negative, political factors exert more influence on market forces, and n is therefore less than 1, and $F + aW/w$ becomes a necessary substitute for qE/r. W. L. Hansen et al., "Forecasting the Market for New Ph.D. Economists," American Economic Review, 70 (March 1980), pp. 49–63, offers a much more elaborate wage-based model. It is, however, entirely a market model, making no distinction between conditions in which political pressures might influence responses.

Table 1.15

Projections of Average Annual New Career Openings for College Teachers of the Humanities, 1980–2000 (thousands)[a]

Year	English	Modern languages	History	Philosophy	Total
		Total openings			
1980–1982	.8–.9	.4–.5	.3–.4	.1–.2	1.3–2.0
1983–1985	.2–.7	.1–.4	.1–.3	.05–.1	.6–1.7
1986–1988	.1–.6	.1–.3	.05–.3	.02–.1	.2–1.3
1989–1991	.2–.8	.1–.5	.1–.4	.04–.2	.5–1.8
1992–1994	.2–.9	.1–.5	.1–.4	.04–.2	.5–2.0
1995–1997	.3–1.1	.2–.6	.1–.5	.06–.2	.7–2.4
1998–2000	.8–2.5	.4–1.4	.4–1.2	.1–.5	1.7–5.4
1980–1990	.3–.8	.2–.5	.2–.4	.06–.2	.8–1.8
1980–1995	.3–.8	.2–.5	.1–.4	.05–.2	.7–1.9
1980–2000	.4–1.1	.2–.6	.2–.5	.07–.2	.8–2.5
		Full-time openings			
1980–1982	.6–.7	.3–.4	.3–.3	.1–.1	1.2–1.4
1983–1985	.2–.3	.1–.2	.1–.2	.03–.1	.3–.8
1986–1988	.04–.2	.02–.1	.02–.1	.01–.04	.1–.5
1989–1991	.1–.4	.1–.2	.1–.2	.02–.07	.3–.8
1992–1994	.1–.4	.1–.2	.1–.2	.02–.1	.3–.9
1995–1997	.2–.6	.1–.3	.1–.3	.03–.1	.4–1.3
1998–2000	.5–1.6	.3–.9	.3–.8	.1–.3	1.2–3.5
1980–1990	.3–.4	.1–.3	.1–.2	.04–.1	.6–1.0
1980–1995	.2–.4	.1–.2	.1–.2	.04–.1	.5–.9
1980–2000	.3–.6	.1–.4	.1–.3	.04–.1	.6–1.4

[a] See notes for Tables 1.8 and 1.14.

4-year colleges where schedules and other demands often preclude scholarly research and writing. If faculty numbers are sustained because average faculty wages go down, even professorships in select colleges and universities could lose attractiveness in the eyes of all would-be scholars except those with private means. Hence, without presuming actually to forecast any numbers, we suggest that prudent planning by

How Many Can Teach?

Table 1.16

Index Projections of Job Openings and/or Salary Levels in College Teaching, 1981–2000 (1980 = 100)[a]

Year	Low range	High range
1981	98	99
1982	98	100
1983	98	100
1984	94	97
1985	92	97
1986	90	96
1987	91	97
1988	98	102
1989	95	101
1990	89	98
1991	85	96
1992	84	96
1993	86	97
1994	88	99
1995	85	98
1996	87	99
1997	89	100
1998	93	102
1999	97	103
2000	98	104

[a] For explanation, see text, pp. 29–30, and note 12. The table uses low and high enrollment projections from Table 1.7 and an assumption that the low-range projections are accompanied by an increase from 50 to 70% in the proportion of college and university revenues available for faculty wages and directly affected by enrollment changes; the high-range projections are accompanied by a corresponding decrease in that proportion.

graduate departments, by counselors of graduating seniors, and by anyone contemplating graduate work should assume that, at least through the mid-1990s, the average number of career openings in college teaching suitable for people intent on scholarship will, give or take 50%, be in the neighborhood of 300 in English, 150 each in modern languages and history, and 50–60 in philosophy. (See Table 1.15.)

2

Who Will Go to Graduate School? Why? Where?

As openings in college teaching dwindle, will numbers of people taking graduate training go down? If so, how much? From the mid-1960s through the 1970s, first-year graduate enrollments in literary studies, history, and philosophy were between 30,000 and 50,000, and total graduate enrollments were between 60,000 and 85,000. Output of Ph.D.'s was 3000–4000 a year, approximately matching numbers of new career openings for college teachers. In the 1980s and 1990s, will graduate enrollments and final numbers of humanities Ph.D.'s plummet to match a much lower level of demand for college teachers?

At least for the first half of the 1980s, it is almost certain that new Ph.D.'s will exceed demand in the academic labor market, for well into the 1980s humanities Ph.D.'s will be predominantly people who started graduate work in the 1970s. The *median* time to a humanities Ph.D. exceeds 7 years. Because many students take some time out, the median time from B.A. to Ph.D. is around 10 years.[1] Since most professors and students did not notice the prospective drop in demand

[1] As of 1978, the median number of years from B.A. to Ph.D. and as a registered doctoral student were as follows: for English, 9.9 and 7.4; for modern languages, 10.4 and 7.3; for history, 10.5 and 7.7; and for philosophy, 10.1 and 7.0. American Council on Education, *1980 Fact Book for Academic Administrators* (Washington, D.C., 1980), p. 143.

for college teachers prior to the mid-1970s, applications to and enrollments in doctoral programs did not begin to fall off until late in the decade.[2] At the beginning of the 1980s about 60,000 remain in the pipeline.

For the first part of the 1980s, therefore, an estimate of numbers of Ph.D.'s is largely an estimate of how degree completion rates will be affected by the actual or prospective downturn in the academic job market. The basic question is this: How many will drop out? An estimate for years beyond the mid-1980s turns on the answer to a two-part question: How many new students will enter Ph.D. programs, and how many of them will complete the degree? Whatever the total numbers of Ph.D.'s in the 1980s and 1990s, where will they come from— all schools, only the better schools, only the poorer schools?

Unlike questions about numbers of teaching jobs, questions about numbers and characteristics of graduate students cannot be addressed by straightforward statistical projections. It is true that, over the past quarter-century, some rough correspondences have obtained between numbers of B.A.'s in the humanities and numbers of first-year graduate students in those fields. In the mid-1950s, approximately 5 B.A.'s out of every 20 went on to graduate school. In the 1960s, 8 out of 20 did so. In the 1970s, the proportion retreated to 6–7 out of 20. Meanwhile, however, there was a significant increase in numbers of graduate students who either did not complete the Ph.D. or stretched out the completion time. At the beginning of the 1960s, there was 1 Ph.D. in the humanities for every 6–7 students enrolled a half-dozen years earlier as first-year graduate students. By the mid-1970s, the corresponding

[2] The first drop occurred in 1977–1978, when graduate enrollments in humanities in Ph.D.-granting institutions fell off 1.4% (down 3.7% in public institutions but up 4.7% in private institutions). *Chronicle of Higher Education,* 24 July 1978, p. 8. After remaining comparatively steady in 1979–1980, the figures rose by 1.1% in 1980–1981 (1.0% public, and 1.3% private). *Ibid.,* 10 November 1980, p. 9.

ratio was 1 Ph.D. to every 12–13 first-year students. (See Table 2.1.)

From these trends, it is possible to make projections, but only within a very broad band. If college enrollments and proportions of students in the humanities fall within the boundaries projected in the previous chapter, then in nearly every year there will be many more humanities Ph.D.'s than there are career openings in college teaching, unless the proportions of first-year graduate enrollments and of graduate students completing the Ph.D. drop below any levels known since World War II. As Table 2.2 indicates, it appears that the "surplus" English, modern language, history, and philosophy Ph.D.'s could run well over 25,000. If so, the figure would actually be much larger, for many of the career openings would go to people without Ph.D.'s. Although the birthrate can be said largely to determine college enrollments and enrollments in turn largely to determine openings in college teaching, numbers of B.A.'s merely contribute to setting an upper limit on numbers of first-year graduate students and numbers of first-year graduate students to setting an upper limit on Ph.D.'s. They are not controlling factors.

To guess how many B.A.'s will go on to graduate school and how many will complete Ph.D.'s, one has to make assumptions about attitudes and motives. If people pursue graduate training in the humanities primarily to prepare for careers as teachers, then evidence of poor job prospects in academe should shut off the flow fairly rapidly. If they enter graduate school primarily for other reasons but complete the Ph.D. chiefly to pursue employment in teaching, then graduate enrollments might remain high but fewer and fewer students will stay to earn their diplomas. On the other hand, if nonvocational motives are strong all the way through, then trends in numbers of both graduate students and Ph.D.'s might correspond only faintly to trends in the academic labor market. The mix of motives could also influence student choices of

Table 2.1
B.A.'s, First-Time Graduate Enrollments, and Ph.D.'s in English, Modern Languages, History, and Philosophy, 1954–1978

Year	B.A.'s[a]	First-year graduate enrollments[b]	Total graduate enrollments[b]	Ph.D.'s	Ratios	
					First-year enrollments to B.A.'s	Ph.D.'s to first-year enrollments 6 years earlier
1954	27,000 (9)	7,000	14,300	1006	1:3.9	n.a.
1960	43,600 (11)	n.a.	30,600	1072	n.a.	1:6.5
1962	53,100 (14)	22,400	38,100	1204	1:2.4	n.a.
1965	80,400 (16)	n.a.	59,200	1831	n.a.	n.a.
1966	87,900 (17)	38,900	64,000	1970	1:2.3	n.a.
1968	108,300 (17)	43,300	75,100	2576	1:2.5	1:8.7
1970	130,400 (16)	49,000	84,700	3311	1:2.7	n.a.
1971	129,200 (15)	45,500	79,600	3641	1:2.8	n.a.
1972	126,600 (14)	43,200	76,700	3907	1:2.9	1:10.0
1973	120,700 (13)	39,300	73,600	4171	1:3.0	1:10.5
1974	111,500 (12)	38,900	71,900	4128	1:2.9	1:10.5
1975	97,100 (10)	36,100	68,900	3919	1:2.7	1:11.9
1976	86,300 (9)	34,000	63,300	3833	1:3.1	1:12.8
1977	78,200 (8)	n.a.	n.a.	3394	n.a.	1:13.4
1978	71,500 (8)	n.a.	n.a.	3071	n.a.	1:14.1

Sources: National Center for Education Statistics, *Digest of Education Statistics*, and *The Condition of Education* (1980).
[a] Numbers in parentheses are percentages of B.A.'s in all fields.
[b] n.a. = data not available.

Table 2.2

Alternative Projections of B.A.'s, First-Time Graduate Enrollments, and Ph.D.'s in English, Modern Languages, History, and Philosophy, and Comparisons with Projections of Career Openings in College Teaching, 1980–2000[a]

Year	B.A.'s	Annual averages (thousands)		New career openings in college teaching (full-time)	Deficit or surplus
		First-time graduate enrollments	Ph.D.'s		
1980–1982	70–71	23–24	2.3–2.6	1.2–1.4	(1.4)–(.9)[b]
1983–1985	65–72	20–24	1.7–1.8	.3–.8	(1.5)–(.9)
1986–1988	58–69	18–23	1.5–1.7	.1–.5	(1.6)–(1.0)
1989–1991	53–68	15–23	1.4–1.7	.3–.8	(1.4)–(.6)
1992–1994	49–67	14–22	1.3–1.8	.3–.9	(1.5)–(.4)
1995–1997	45–66	12–22	1.1–1.8	.4–1.3	(1.4)–.2
1998–2000	45–72	11–24	.9–2.0	1.2–3.5	(.8)–2.6
Totals			30.6–40.2	11.4–27.6	(28.8)–(3.0)

[a] Figures are based on enrollment and faculty projections in Tables 1.7 and 1.15. It is assumed that B.A.'s remain 10% of full-time-equivalent enrollments, humanities B.A.'s remain 10–12% of the total, first-time graduate enrollments remain 25–33.3% of the previous year's B.A.'s, and the ratio between Ph.D.'s and first-time graduate enrollments 6 years earlier remains between 1:15 and 1:12.

[b] Numbers in parentheses indicate negative values.

graduate schools. At this point, therefore, we have to turn from demographic data to data drawn from survey research.

In the mid-1970s the Higher Education Research Institute (HERI) conducted a questionnaire survey of approximately 4000 graduate students in English, French, Spanish, history, and philosophy. The two of us helped design the questionnaires and analyze the results. The students were located at 40 different universities, 20 of which were the leading producers of Ph.D.'s in these fields and 20 of which represented other large producers. We visited most of these universities, interviewing in all about 500 graduate students.[3]

Of the questionnaire respondents, approximately one-fourth were first-year graduate students, most of whom had enrolled with full knowledge that the outlook in college teaching was dark. Although most of these students thought their own prospects better than those of the typical student, the whole group of respondents rated as poor or uncertain the chances of any graduate student's landing any type of job. (See Table 2.3.) Their attitudes and opinions are therefore those of people aware of the trends described in Chapter 1. Students who

[3] Lewis C. Solmon, Nancy L. Ochsner, and Margo-Lea Hurwicz, in *Alternative Careers for Humanities Ph.D.'s: Perspectives of Students and Graduates* (New York: Praeger, 1980) present a detailed technical report on this survey. It was designed in 1974–1975 by the Solmon team, ourselves, and the late Allan Cartter. The 40 universities were *The University of Arizona, Boston University, Bryn Mawr, California (Berkeley)*, UCLA, *University of Cincinnati*, Chicago, *Claremont, University of Colorado, Columbia, University of Connecticut, Cornell*, University of Florida, *Georgetown, Harvard*, Illinois (Urbana), *University of Indiana, Johns Hopkins*, University of Kansas, Kent State, *University of Kentucky*, Michigan State, *Michigan (Ann Arbor)*, University of Minnesota, *NYU, North Carolina (Chapel Hill)*, Northwestern, *Notre Dame, Ohio State, University of Pennsylvania, Princeton, USC, Stanford*, Suny (Buffalo), *Texas (Austin), Tulane, Vanderbilt, Washington (Seattle)*, Wisconsin (Madison), and *Yale*. Interviews were conducted at each of the italicized institutions. In most cases, the interviews were with panels of 4–12 graduate students from a single department or discipline selected by the department head, the director of graduate studies, or the graduate dean to represent students at all stages of graduate work.

Table 2.3

Humanities Graduate Students' Perceptions of the Academic Job Market
(percentages)

	Perception of prospects as:		
	Good	Uncertain	Poor
Job prospects for the typical graduate student in his or her field ($N = 3789$)			
Teaching positions in the most prestigious 4-year colleges and universities	2	6	92
Teaching positions in other 4-year colleges and universities	6	21	71
Teaching positions in 2-year colleges	19	37	43
Government positions	13	33	52
Business positions	10	25	63
	Better	Same	Worse
Personal job prospects compared with those of other graduate students in field ($N = 3669$)	61	32	7
Personal job prospects in academe (teaching, research, administration, and so on) compared with those of the typical graduate student at same institution ($N = 2669$)			
In other humanities	30	49	19
In the social sciences	13	36	49
In the physical sciences	4	15	81
In the biological sciences	4	14	80

were interviewed certainly knew of them, for we discussed them in detail with each panel.

The survey and interview results may therefore say something about the graduate student population of the future. Half were men, half women. Three-quarters were in their twenties, and most of the rest were in their thirties. Half were single; half were or had been married. Not surprisingly, they had many academic honors. More than half had graduated cum laude or better. More than a third had held some kind of merit-based scholarship in college. Almost a quarter belonged to Phi Beta Kappa. On the whole, however, they had not done much extracurricularly. Only one out of eight or nine had been involved in student journalism, debate, dramatics, or music; fewer still had held any elective class office. These returns were consistent with the stereotype of graduate students as "grinds."

The majority of these students had not just floated from college to graduate school. Over half had interrupted their education for a year or more, usually between college and graduate school. For the most part, however, they had not been exploring possible careers. Students who were interviewed told of clerking in stores, waiting on tables, or otherwise earning money in routine jobs not unlike those they had held in summers while in college. Most had thought of themselves as taking time off from school rather than trying out an occupation. They planned all along to enroll in graduate school and gave little thought to alternatives. In the HERI survey sample, fewer than 1 in 6 even considered a professional school. Only about 1 in 20 thought seriously of going to work for government or entering business. (See Table 2.4.)

In a different sample of graduate students surveyed by the American Council on Education at the end of the 1960s, three-quarters of doctoral candidates in the humanities were from families at or below the median-income level. One in five came from a working-class background. The percentages were higher than among students in professional schools, and, although nearly all said they were in graduate school for intellectual growth, 70% added that they wanted to increase earnings and almost half said that they wanted a prestigious job. These returns suggested a high proportion of students who expected a graduate degree to improve their social and economic status.

In the later HERI sample only one-fifth described their families as below the middle-income level. Almost a third char-

Table 2.4
Humanities Graduate Students' Consideration of Alternatives to Entering Graduate School[a]

	How considered (percentages)	
Job alternative	Very seriously	Not at all
Professional school	15	52
Elementary- or secondary-school teaching	15	51
Graduate school in another discipline	12	53
Public service (Peace Corps, etc.)	6	60
Job in government	6	62
Job in business	4	67
Administrative work in college or university	4	71

[a] $N = 3852$.

acterized their families as upper middle in income or even as rich. Since the questions were not the same, the returns are not perfectly comparable. Half of the HERI respondents put their families in the middle-income group, and some proportion would, if asked, have placed them below the median. In the earlier sample, only one-third of humanities graduate students had fathers with a college degree. In the later sample, the proportion was one-half. To be sure, the family income estimates are not comparable, and allowance has to be made for a general increase in numbers of college graduates old enough to be parents of graduate students. The two sets of data nevertheless suggest that the population of doctoral candidates in the humanities may have changed. The proportion who were upwardly mobile, either economically or socially, may have diminished as dark prospects in the academic job market began to be publicized. (See Table 2.5.)

Comparisons also suggest a decrease in the proportion of students entering humanities graduate programs for reasons other than self-gratification. Though both groups identified "intellectual growth" or "knowledge for personal satisfaction"

Table 2.5

Characteristics of Humanities Graduate Students, 1970 and 1976

	1970 sample[a]		1976 sample
	All graduate students (N = 33,119)	Humanities graduate students (N = 4985)	Humanities graduate students (N = 3884)
Median age	27	26	27
Married (%)	58	56	40
College-graduate fathers (%)	34	35	51
College-graduate mothers (%)	24	27	36
Parents "financially comfortable" (%)	72	74	
Parents middle income or higher (%)			80
Reasons for being in graduate school or important motivations for pursuing an advanced degree (%)			
Intellectual growth	97	97	
Intrinsic interest	82	90	
Expansion of knowledge for personal satisfaction			90
Desire to serve mankind	74	75	
Desire to increase earnings	75	70	
Pecuniary advantages			20
Job requirements	64	65	
Degree needed for position as college teacher			84
Desire for more independent work life			67

(*continued*)

Table 2.5
(*continued*)

	1970 sample[a]		1976 sample
	All graduate students (N = 33,119)	Humanities graduate students (N = 4985)	Humanities graduate students (N = 3884)
Desire to change society	61	58	
Desire for prestigious job	57	45	
More rapid career advancement			25
Desire to find oneself	30	35	
Peer-group encouragement			15
Delay of career choice			10

[a] John A. Creager, *The American Graduate Student: A Normative Study,* American Council on Education Research Reports, Vol. 6, No. 5 (1971).

as the leading motive, the later sample had no clear counterpart for the 50–70% in the earlier group acknowledging money or social prestige as also important. Though 6 out of 7 did check "necessary for college teaching" as an additional factor, fewer than 1 in 4 put an appropriate mark beside "pecuniary advantages" or "rapid career advancement." When asked to indicate reasons for their choice of a particular field of study, 97% selected "intellectual satisfaction," but only 7% chose "better employment prospects." (See Table 2.6.)

When interviewed, many students of the 1970s spoke of deliberately forgoing material rewards. "I've found that it is very important for me to love what I do," said a man studying Romance languages at Princeton. "This is more important than money." From one of a group of doctoral candidates at Georgetown came the comment, "Anyone in the room could accept a job that paid $90,000 a year, but by choosing philosophy we have taken ourselves out of competition for such jobs."

Table 2.6
Humanities Graduate Students' Motives for Choosing a Particular Field[a]

Motive	Percentage
Intellectual satisfaction	97
Special aptitude	83
Undergraduate major	65
Offered breadth	52
Good department, location	47
Necessary for career advancement	32
Faculty advice	29
Flexible course offering	21
Attractive financial offer	20
Family encouragement	16
Better chance for admission	14
Rapid completion of Ph.D.	7
Better employment prospects	7
Peer-group influence	5

[a] N = 3918.

The HERI survey results can be interpreted as showing in themselves an increase in the proportion of students doing graduate work just because they enjoy it, for newly enrolled students put more emphasis on "knowledge for personal satisfaction" than did more advanced students, and they put significantly less emphasis on the use of the degree for a career in teaching. (See Table 2.7.) Among first-year students, 1 out of 10 expressed regret at having enrolled in graduate school, and only 1 out of 6 said that, if doing it over, he or she would go to a professional school. Among "A.B.D.'s" ("All But Dissertation"—people who completed all requirements for the Ph.D. except the dissertation) approximately twice as many expressed similar views, and 3 out of 10 wished they had studied law, medicine, or business. (See Table 2.8.)

The sample of more advanced students, to be sure, included many who entered when demand for college teachers seemed high. "I was *encouraged* to go into medieval history," complained one man at Berkeley. "I was told there were lots of

Table 2.7

Humanities Graduate Students' Motives for Pursuing an Advanced Degree,
by Levels (percentages)

Motive	First-year students (N = 989)	Advanced students (N = 1559)	A.B.D.'s (N = 1336)
Knowledge for personal satisfaction	91	90	88
Desire to become a college teacher	74	85	91
More independent work life	57	69	73
More rapid career advancement	24	24	26
Pecuniary advantages	20	19	20
Peer-group encouragement	14	14	16
Delaying of career choice	15	10	6

jobs." Such people were understandably rueful. The evidence of their higher level of discontent, however, strengthens the inference that the 1970s saw a decrease in the percentage of humanities graduate students who were career-oriented.

Two magnets continuing to pull people into humanities doctoral programs by the late 1970s were the subject matter—

Table 2.8

What Humanities Graduate Students Would Do if Reconsidering Entering
Graduate School

Option	First-year students (N = 972)	Advanced students (N = 1532)	A.B.D.'s (N = 1319)
Take more courses in another area, but continue in major field	33	34	37
Change or broaden the range of career goals, but enter present program	26	25	30
Change institution but not field	25	25	21
Work for a professional degree (e.g., law) instead	17	22	30
Change major field	15	21	23
Not attend graduate school	10	12	19

the delightful prospect of reading more great literature, learning more history, or playing with ideas—and the setting. At Columbia a woman who had done her undergraduate degree in one of England's redbrick universities declared that she had no interest in teaching and was in graduate school only because she liked "the life-style and also the intellectual side." A fourth-year student in English at Princeton said, "What draws us all to these programs is the quality of life. . . . I'm just enjoying myself." More than a dozen other students expressed agreement, one adding: "Many of us are in it to maintain a certain life-style, to prolong the university setting."

Such testimony helps to explain why, even of the A.B.D.'s, 7 out of 10 said that, if they had it to do over again, they would still pursue the Ph.D. Also, however, it encourages an inference that more and more of the men and women entering humanities doctoral programs may be doing so as dilettantes, prolonging undergraduate life rather than seriously equipping themselves to be producers, purveyors, or treasurers of humanistic learning. More and more would then be represented by the student of English at Yale who defined his only goals as "autonomy and personhood" or at best the student of history at the University of Connecticut who conceded, "I'm in this as a hobby."

Reinforcing such an impression are three disquieting pieces of evidence. The first is that, though numbers of new humanities graduate students have remained high, they have come from an applicant pool that has been rapidly drying up. In 1970–1971 there were more than 23,000 applications by college seniors for Graduate Record Examinations in literature, history, and philosophy. By 1976–1977 there were only 10,000.[4] For a number of reasons—many graduate departments did not require the examination, the fee had risen in the interval, and

[4] Kenneth M. Deitch, *Some Aspects of the Economics of American Higher Education*, Working Paper for the Sloan Commission on Government and Higher Education (January 1978), p. 68.

the count is of examinations rather than examinees—these numbers do not show that the pool actually shrank by more than half. They do suggest that hosts of college seniors ceased to include graduate study in the humanities among their postgraduate options. The pool of talent became shallower.

The second piece of evidence comes from the HERI survey. Questionnaire responses showed that a large number of students were going for graduate study to institutions that were not as selective as the ones where they earned their B.A.'s. With SAT (Scholastic Aptitude Test) scores of students as a measure, the nation's colleges and universities can be classified according to their academic selectivity. Students in the sample were evenly divided among graduate schools. One-third were in universities where SATs were low, one-third where they were average, and one-third where they were high. Half of them, however, had done their undergraduate work in colleges where SATs ran high, and only a quarter had been in schools where the scores ran low. (See Table 2.9.) Many students, to be sure, may have been turned down by departments that already had strict limits on admissions. One-quarter of those in the early years of graduate work said that they were pleased

Table 2.9
Selectivity of Undergraduate and Graduate Institutions Attended by Humanities Graduate Students[a,b]

	Least selective				Most selective
	(0–999)	(1000–1099)	(1100–1199)	(1200–1299)	(1300+)
Undergraduate degree	9	17	28	25	21
Graduate enrollment	19	15	33	22	11

[a] Selectivity number is median Scholastic Aptitude Test (SAT) plus Mathematical Aptitude Test (MAT) score of entire student body.
[b] $N = 3225$.

with their field of study but wished they were in a different institution. (See Table 2.8.) Even so, for a large number of humanities graduate students the move from college to graduate school involved a move to a less competitive environment.

The third piece of evidence indicates that, although the more recent crop of graduate students seem not to think much about levels of future earnings, they are very responsive to short-term financial incentives. A few students in the survey sample attended institutions such as the University of Chicago, where they had to pay their own way. Most, however, were subsidized by graduate assistantships or university fellowships. Only one in eight had used any savings or borrowed any money to underwrite his or her education. Collectively, they met less than 10% of their expenses with savings, loans, earnings from nonacademic jobs, or even contributions from parents or spouses. Not surprisingly, Phi Beta Kappas and others having many undergraduate honors were those most likely to be heavily supported by their universities. (See Table 2.10.)

Every student who was interviewed said that he or she would not stay in school if forced to borrow. Many indicated that they would not have come at all if they had not been sure that some form of university financial support would materialize no later than the second year. Quite a few testified that their choice of school had turned on the size of a fellowship offer. A Ph.D. candidate in history said he had gone to Columbia "because it offered money." A man in the same field said he had intended to go to law school but "I backed out because I got a good fellowship offer from Princeton." Another historian, admitted by several leading departments, selected Georgetown because, he said, "they offered the most money." Representative of many statements was that of an English Ph.D. candidate at Arizona: "I like what I'm doing and I'm paid to do what I like." Although it is possible that the small minority using savings or borrowing money represent a more dedicated group, analysis of the survey data suggests that they

Table 2.10

How Humanities Graduate Students Finance Their Graduate Training

Source	Percentage of expenses derived from source			
	0	1–40	40–80	80–100
Earnings from academic employment	38	20	18	23
University fellowship	70	11	11	7
Spouse's earnings	74	13	9	3
Family contribution	67	20	7	6
Earnings from nonacademic employment	66	25	5	4
Savings	67	27	3	2
Loans	81	13	5	1

$N = 3982$

	Percentage according to undergraduate awards received					
	0	1	2	3	4	5+
Earnings from academic employment	34	37	38	37	35	35
University fellowship	8	11	13	18	21	21
Spouse's earnings	13	12	11	10	9	10
Family contribution	11	10	10	9	9	11
Earnings from nonacademic employment	11	10	10	9	8	9
Savings	10	7	8	7	6	6
Loans	6	6	5	5	6	5
N	622	792	781	746	506	535

are more likely to be people held in graduate school by family or household pressures or by hope of recovering something from sunk costs.[5]

Taken as a whole, survey and interview data and other pieces of evidence suggest that graduate enrollments in the humanities will remain at higher levels than would be the case if they were strictly responsive to conditions in the academic labor market. Large numbers of people come to graduate school, it appears, for the experience itself. Many are prepared to pursue the experience even if doing so involves going from a good school to one not as good. In a great many cases, the short-term prospect of a fellowship or assistantship exerts allure, despite knowledge that longer-term job prospects are bleak. And the fellowships and assistantships are almost certain to continue, for universities cannot find much cheaper ways of filling out their teaching forces. Consideration of these factors suggests that the population of humanities graduate students should probably be projected as not falling much below 50,000 at any time in the next two decades.

It is by no means clear, to be sure, that an annual increment of over 20,000 first-year graduate students would continue to lead to an annual output of 1500–2000 Ph.D.'s. The fact that

[5] Multiple regression calculations identified some variables associated with the minority's propensity to take out loans or use savings to finance graduate education. (Figures in parentheses are final step betas.) They attended comparatively selective institutions (.173), regarded their own job prospects as better than those of graduate students generally (.090) but not as good as those of their classmates ($-.109$); were committed to their disciplines in the sense of not having seriously considered graduate work in a different field ($-.074$); wished in retrospect that they had studied at a different institution (.084); belonged to the minority that had, at the time of graduating from college, regarded academic administration (.156) or business (.100) as career options. Also, they had comparatively highly educated spouses (.115) and mothers (.052). ($N = 530$; $r^2 = .33$; $F = 13.91067$; $df = 18.511$.) All in all, the picture that emerges is not one of cocky geniuses betting on their ability to succeed despite the odds. See Appendix, Tables A.1–A.3.

20–30% of students in the HERI survey said they would not be in graduate school if they had their lives to live over suggests that many are temperamentally bent on finishing what they start, even if they rue it. As a student of French literature at NYU said, "The Ph.D. is a commitment you make to yourself and you want to get it." Some, of course, could have other motives. A graduate student in English at Johns Hopkins said that he and his fellow students were completing their degrees only because they were afraid to issue from the academic cocoon. He described himself as "lazy and frightened" and accused others of being similarly timid in the face of a world where efforts and rewards took forms other than examinations and grades. In either case, the result would be the same. If, however, the proportion of dilettante students increases, the relative numbers actually getting degrees would drop. Nothing in the available data enables one to go beyond an assertion that numbers of humanities Ph.D.'s awarded through the 1980s and 1990s may fall below 1000 or rise well above 2000 a year.

Nor does existing evidence permit more than speculation concerning the quality of graduate students and Ph.D.'s. Indications that many students go from challenging colleges to less challenging graduate departments, together with evidence that choices by the majority may be strongly influenced by the availability of short-term financial support, give rise to apprehension that there will be not only a diminishing proportion of purposeful would-be scholars but that some—perhaps many—may fail to go to the universities or graduate departments where they could get the most rigorous training. While the Ph.D. boom was on, many institutions enlarged or initiated doctoral programs even though their faculties and research facilities were comparatively weak. A National Board on Graduate Education looked into the possibility that Gresham's law would take effect and concluded reassuringly that the majority of students were applying to and receiving their training in departments with strong and long-established programs.[6] The National Board's evidence came, however, from a period when the National Defense Education Act and National Defense Foreign Language fellowships were numerous. The Ford Foundation was still putting millions into Woodrow Wilson fellowships, and students eligible for these awards had, for practical purposes, freedom to pick their own schools. These conditions subsequently changed.

By the end of the 1970s little government or foundation money was going to humanities doctoral candidates. Most of the money that universities could offer took the form of compensation for teaching. The stronger institutions had less to offer than did the weaker ones. With low student–faculty ratios and with some senior faculty time freed because of the absolute reduction in graduate student numbers, they had diminishing need for teaching assistants. The weaker schools, with higher ratios and previously small graduate enrollments, experienced no such change.

It is not yet clear where humanities graduate students will study in the future. Hoping for an edge in competition for the few college teaching vacancies, serious students could decide to make sacrifices for the sake of getting the best and presumably most salable degrees. It is not implausible, however, that students will simply distribute themselves according to the availability of teaching assistantships, and the result will be that the proportion receiving the best available training will be smaller than in the 1960s and 1970s. The absolute number of truly well-trained humanists could thus drop sharply.

As of the late 1960s, two-thirds of humanities Ph.D.'s were issuing from 25 universities. As of the mid-1970s, the proportion from the top 25 was below 40%. (See Table 2.11.) If this trend should continue, perhaps even stimulated by inter-

---

[6] David W. Breneman, *Graduate School Adjustments to the "New Depression" in Higher Education* (Washington, D.C.: National Board on Graduate Education, 1975).

university competition for cheap graduate-student labor, the proportion from an elite group of schools could be significantly lower, and the proportion of Ph.D.'s adequately trained for scholarship could be correspondingly smaller.

Since long-term openings in college teaching seem sure to be fewer than numbers of new Ph.D.'s, one might infer that Ph.D.'s from elite schools will have the best crack at such jobs. This may not, however, be true. In the first place, as many as half of the openings in college teaching may be reserved for people without the Ph.D, because administrators in 2-year colleges tend to think that non-Ph.D.'s make better teachers.[7] In the second place, a number of teaching jobs for Ph.D.'s will be within virtually closed systems—in state colleges that draw almost all faculty from graduate departments in their own state university, even if those departments are comparatively undistinguished, or in church-related colleges that draw similarly from a single source.

In the third place, the market for teachers in 4-year colleges and universities is actually many markets. An opening in history is not an opening for any historian. It may be limited to a field as narrow as the history of the United States in the Jacksonian period. In a given year, the best Ph.D. from the best department could fail to be hired as a teacher because his or her specialty happened not to be in demand. It seems improbable that more than a third—at most half—of the prospective career openings in college teaching can or will go to humanists with doctorates from the leading graduate departments.

If the central concern is the vitality of humanistic scholarship, two interrelated questions stand out. The first is whether enough talented and purposeful people will seek the training necessary to become scholars. Will the people who might

[7] Frank J. Atelsak and Irene L. Gomberg, *New Full-Time Faculty 1976–1977: Hiring Patterns by Field and Education Attainment*, American Council on Education Higher Education Panel Report No. 38 (1978).

Table 2.11
Universities Training Humanities Ph.D.'s, 1959–1960 and 1973–1974[a]

University	1959–1960			1973–1974		
	Rank	Number of humanities Ph.D.'s	Percentage of all Ph.D.'s	Rank	Number of humanities Ph.D.'s	Percentage of all Ph.D.'s
University of Wisconsin	4	47	4	1	149	4
Columbia	1	128	12	2	145	4
University of Chicago	6	34	3	3	98	2
University of Michigan	5	35	3	4	88	2
Illinois (Urbana)	9	28	3	5	87	2
California (Berkeley)	8	29	3	6	82	2
Harvard	2	73	7	7	81	2
University of Indiana	12	22	2	8	75	2
Stanford	10–11	18	2	9	69	2
California (UCLA)	14	21	2	10	66	2
Yale	3	65	6	11	63	2
Texas (Austin)	19–22	15	1	12	58	1
University of Pennsylvania	10–11	23	2	13	52	1
University of Virginia	< 25	10	1	14	51	1
Fordham	23–24	14	1	15	50	1
University of Minnesota	7	31	3	16	49	1
Princeton	10–11	23	2	17	45	1
Brown	19–22	15	1	18–19	44	1
University of Iowa	18	19	2	18–19	44	1
Florida State	< 25	< 10	< 1	20	42	1
University of Washington	16	21	2	21	41	1
California (Santa Barbara)	< 25	< 10	< 1	22–23	40	< 1
Cornell	< 25	11	1	22–23	40	< 1
Duke	< 25	< 10	< 1	24	39	< 1
Massachusetts (Amherst)	< 25	< 10				

University of Kansas	< 25	< 10	< 1	26	36	< 1
Michigan State	25	< 10	< 1	27	34	< 1
CUNY	25	< 10	< 1	28	32	< 1
University of Colorado	25	< 10	< 1	29	31	< 1
Tulane	25	< 10	1	30–32	30	< 1
Georgetown	25	< 10	1	30–32	30	< 1
Syracuse	25	< 10	1	30–32	30	< 1
Kent State	25	< 10	1	33	29	< 1
Vanderbilt	25	< 10	1	34	28	< 1
Brandeis	< 25	< 10	1	35–36	27	< 1
USC	23–24	14	1	35–36	27	< 1
University of Maryland	25	< 10	< 1	37–38	26	< 1
University of Connecticut	25	< 10	< 1	37–38	26	< 1
Johns Hopkins	17	20	2	39–40	25	< 1
University of Kentucky	< 25	< 10	< 1	39–40	25	< 1
Case Western Reserve	25	< 10	< 1	< 40	24	< 1
University of Georgia	25	< 10	< 1	< 40	24	< 1
Boston Univ.	13	21	2	< 40	22	< 1
LSU	< 25	< 10	< 1	< 40	22	< 1
St. Louis University	19–22	15	1	< 40	22	< 1
Catholic University	19–22	15	1	< 40	21	< 1
University of Florida	25	13	1	< 40	18	< 1
Bryn Mawr	< 25	11	1	40	16	< 1
25 leaders		759	71		1635	40
40 leaders					2071	50
All universities		1074	100		4128	100

Source: U.S. Office of Education, *Earned Degrees Conferred, 1959–1960* (1962) and *1973–1974* (1976).
[a] Includes Ph.D.'s in English, modern languages, history, and philosophy.

shape understanding of literature, history, and philosophy for the next generation pursue careers in business or government without ever mastering the basic skills and information needed for scholarly research? The second question concerns those talented and purposeful people who do obtain scholarly training. If not all of them—perhaps, indeed, only a few of them—can find secure careers in academe, what are the chances of their being able to contribute to scholarship from bases elsewhere in society?

The two questions are intricately related because the attractiveness of graduate training to people with potential for scholarship may well turn on their impressions concerning opportunities and possibilities in the event that they do not spend their lives as professors. The next subjects to which we turn are therefore the experiences of humanities Ph.D.'s who have in the past adopted nonteaching careers, and prospects for those who do so in the future.

3

Humanists Outside Academe

Since the historic pattern for 9 out of 10 humanities Ph.D.'s has been simply to move from one side of the podium to the other, the number not in teaching careers has never been large. Of 60,000 whom the National Research Council could locate in 1977, all but 4800 (8%) were employed by schools or colleges.[1]

These 4800 were mavericks. Receiving their Ph.D.'s when the degree carried with it virtual title to a teaching job, they were for the most part people who chose not to teach. Even so, evidence about them is suggestive. It says something about how graduate training in the humanities has been used or not used in lines of work other than teaching. It also says something about possibilities for continued scholarly work by people whose places of work are not classrooms.

Most of the evidence comes from a second HERI survey, again supplemented by interviews.[2] The objective was to poll a significant sample of Ph.D.'s in English, French, Spanish, history, and philosophy and compare the answers of non-

[1] National Research Council, Commission on Human Resources, *Employment of Humanities Ph.D.'s* (Washington, D.C., 1980), p. 24.

[2] Technical analysis is in Lewis C. Solmon, Nancy L. Ochsner, and Margo-Lea Hurwicz, *Alternative Careers for Humanities Ph.D.'s: Perspectives of Students and Graduates* (New York: Praeger, 1980).

academics with those of academics matching them in fields, age, sex, and other characteristics.

The original plan called for surveying Ph.D.'s from the 40 universities whose graduate students were simultaneously being questioned. This plan had to be abandoned. Graduate departments knew only the addresses of Ph.D.'s who were teachers. A sample of nonacademics had to be rounded out by posting notices at professional association meetings, searching the computerized personnel rosters of cooperative corporations and government agencies, and placing in the book review section of the Sunday *New York Times* a large paid ad headed: "Are You Now or Have You Ever Been a Humanities Ph.D.?" The ad included a coupon order for a questionnaire.

These efforts produced 1200 responses from Ph.D.'s or A.B.D.'s not working as teachers. A comparable sample of teachers was easily found. Alike in most characteristics other than type of work, the two groups together were similar to the HERI sample of graduate students. They were, of course, older and scattered across the age spectrum. Coming from generations that had felt less affirmative-action pressure, the two groups were both about three-quarters male instead of being half male and half female. Not surprisingly, in view of their age, a larger proportion—approximately 80%—were or had been married. Almost half had spouses who worked. Though both groups included many from the population that the American Council on Education had surveyed at the end of the 1960s, they did not have its characteristic family income distribution or upwardly mobile appearance. Instead, the proportions from rich, middle-income, and poor families were almost the same as in the contemporaneous graduate student sample—heavily weighted toward upper middle. In academic honors and college extracurricular activities, the Ph.D.'s also resembled the students. Twenty-two percent were Phi Beta Kappas. The majority had been "grinds."

Of those not employed as teachers, a large number worked for academic institutions. The survey respondents were therefore divided into four groups. First, there was the "faculty" group. Larger in number than the comparison sample of people not teaching, this group consisted of about 1600 people, somewhat fewer than 100 of whom were teaching below the college level. The other groups were "academic administrators," "other academic" (a miscellany dominated by college librarians), and "nonacademic." The last group exceeded 800 and thus formed about two-thirds of all those not employed as teachers. Offsetting possible distortion due to inclusion of secondary-school teachers among faculty was inclusion in this nonacademic group of somewhat fewer than 100 who had no employment at all, mostly people going dispiritedly from one fruitless academic job interview to another.

For the guidance of graduate students and new Ph.D.'s voluntarily or involuntarily considering careers other than teaching, the evidence is illuminating chiefly because it cannot be generalized. When looking back on their time in graduate school, few humanities Ph.D.'s believe that it enhanced their imaginativeness. (See Table 3.2.) Anyone who hears students or professors discussing "alternative careers" has confirming evidence, for the range of possibilities seldom runs much beyond librarian, archivist, or curator, with little note that these professions have their own entry systems and surpluses of talent. Teaching at the secondary or elementary level sometimes crops up, despite the fact that the students not to be in college in future years are already not filling chairs in schoolrooms, and despite barriers posed by certification requirements, union rules, and union–school board contracts. The survey sample of nonacademics suggests how much more varied are the types of jobs that humanities Ph.D.'s have actually had.

The group did include some who entered another profession by taking another degree. Among the nonacademics were 15 lawyers, 15 Protestant ministers, 2 priests, 2 nuns, a monk, a rabbi, and an Episcopalian bishop. Such professionals, however, formed a distinct minority. Most of the nonacademics had jobs that required little or no additional specialized training.

Some had careers as researchers, employed by federal executive departments, the Congressional Reference Service, or state or local governments. The largest single collection of humanities Ph.D.'s engaged in research appeared to be in the Central Intelligence Agency. Others did research for private companies. At IBM's austere headquarters in Armonk, New York, for example, a philosophy Ph.D. who started out as a poet sat alone in a study seeing if he could dream up chains of logic computers could not follow.

Many humanities Ph.D.'s were editors or writers. A few were at unsurprising addresses such as the University of Chicago Press. Others were with journals such as *Crawdaddy West* or with newsmagazines or newspapers. A still larger number were connected with corporate house organs like those of Westinghouse, Exxon, and Eastman Kodak. Others listed themselves as staff writers for such concerns as Blue Cross–Blue Shield. Le Anne Schreiber, once a doctoral candidate in the English department at Harvard, went by age 33 from writing about international politics for *Time* to editing *Women Sports* magazine to being the sports editor of the *New York Times*, where from 1978 to 1980 she directed a department of 55 reporters and editors. Now deputy editor of the *Times Book Review*, she says, "I believe that the two things I have to sell are a highly developed critical intelligence and an ability to teach and write. I just had to convince people that I could translate these skills from an academic to a nonacademic environment."

Of the 800 nonacademics, one-fourth were administrators or managers. Their employers included Xerox, Cummins Electric, Pillsbury, Gimbels, General Motors, Korvettes, the Ford Foundation, and the National Endowment for the Humanities. (Academic administrators were a category apart.) One Ph.D. was vice-president for lending at a commercial bank, another a senior vice-president in a computer company, another the proprietor of a men's clothing store, yet another the president of a wine company. More than a score were section heads, office directors, or the like in U.S. government agencies. Two were or had been U.S. senators.

Finally, apart from a cluster of Ph.D.'s marking time as cabdrivers, gardeners, tree trimmers, house painters, and waiters (one a very well-off French-speaking headwaiter), there were salesmen and saleswomen. During interviews with students, mention of this occupation usually provoked retching sounds and references to Willie Loman. Some humanists who had tried it, however, echoed an outspoken graduate student at the University of Pennsylvania who protested a fellow student's saying that he could not imagine thus compromising himself. "That's a lot of crap," she said. "I come from a business family. I play the same damn games my father does. We are trying to sell education now. We are selling ourselves all the time. Do you think people need literature any more than a paper towel?" Arousing interest in a product, said several humanities Ph.D.'s, was not inherently different from arousing interest in a poem or a period of history or an idea. Often, it involved chiefly explanation very similar to good classroom teaching. And some people selling on commission claimed to have more control than college teachers over their hours, days, and seasons of work.

Among the humanities Ph.D.'s whom we interviewed were Robert Brawer and David Matthew. Brawer's degree, in medieval English literature, was from the University of Chicago. He taught for several years at the University of Wisconsin, was recommended for promotion, but was denied it because the line was not funded. Concluding that he did not want any of the other jobs then open, he made use of personal connections to get into the marketing department of Maidenform Inc. To his surprise and pleasure, he found the analytical problems in his new job not unlike those in his academic field. "Market research," he said, "is like any other kind of research. I'm very satisfied." He also commented that "the ability to sell is intimately related to the ability to teach."

Though Brawer had clearly left his academic discipline, he continued to teach part-time at night and to present scholarly papers. David Matthew became an entrepreneur and salesman halfway between academe and the world outside. A Ph.D. in

English from Columbia, he taught for a time and truly enjoyed teaching. He became bored, however, with repeating the same material year after year, and he concluded that he did not yearn to produce the type or quantity of publication necessary for success in a prestigious university. After a long search for a nonteaching job, he found one that excited him—devising and marketing business training seminars and programmed learning systems. He said that in working on and selling these systems he was doing at least as much as he could as a professor to use his training in the humanities for educational purposes. And he added: "The difference between the university and business is that in business if you do a good job at what you're paid to do, you get promoted."

Interviews with people such as Brawer and Matthew, together with the survey data, convinced the two of us that the business world had many more openings for humanities Ph.D.'s than the large majority of either graduate students or professors even suspected. We did not suppose that humanities Ph.D.'s were any better suited for business than for government—federal, state, or local—or for employment by foundations or health-care facilities or other such in-between organizations. We did observe, however, that, largely out of prejudice compounded by ignorance, graduate students were disposed not to think of business as an alternative to academe. Aware that the private sector is where the majority of challenging and well-paid jobs are to be found, we sounded out some corporate hiring officers but found them almost equally prejudiced. They seemed to assume that humanities graduate students had made a definite decision against a business career and also that they were unsuited for such careers.

We thought that the barrier of misunderstanding could and should be broken. The New York State Regents agreed to sponsor a demonstration project. Funds came from the National Endowment for the Humanities, the Rockefeller Foundation, and the Exxon Education Foundation, and from companies as diverse as AT&T, Time Inc., the Prudential and

Metropolitan insurance companies, Dupont, Federated Department Stores, Pfizer, Sun Chemical, General Motors, and Ford. The NYU Graduate School of Business Administration agreed to offer a 7-week summer "Careers in Business" program.

In each of two successive summers, 45–50 outstanding humanities Ph.D.'s and near-Ph.D.'s were recruited for this program. Once corporate personnel officers saw the quality of these people—many of whom had served several years as assistant professors—more than threescore major companies lined up to interview them. Alumni were hired for jobs ranging from administrator of a corporate foundation to analyst of economic forecasts for an investment management concern to account executive for an advertising agency to line manager in an insurance company. On the average, they were starting at salaries comparable to those of M.B.A.'s and far above those standard for junior faculty.

That humanities Ph.D.'s can find careers in business appealing and that business concerns can in turn see in humanities Ph.D.'s an untapped reservoir of talent is witnessed by the fact that NYU continued its 7-week summer orientation program, supporting it through a combination of tuition and corporate donations. Further testimony is imitation of the NYU program by Harvard, the Wharton School at the University of Pennsylvania, the University of Virginia, UCLA, and elsewhere.[3] As a result of the demonstration project and its effects, students have had before them more role models to challenge their prejudices, and corporate hiring officers have had fresh examples proving that their assumptions at least require room for exceptions.

The chief point that emerges from survey data, interviews,

[3] Regents of the University of the State of New York, *Careers in Business* (Albany, N.Y., 1978), *Careers in Business, 1979* (Albany, N.Y., 1979), and NYU Graduate School of Business Administration, *Careers in Business, 1980* (New York, 1980).

and the results of the demonstration project is that humanities Ph.D.'s and graduate students have open to them career opportunities that are at least as numerous and varied as those open to liberal arts B.A.'s. Graduate training does not in itself disqualify anyone for any job. All that people with such training have to do is to define themselves in terms of their general capabilities, not their dissertation subjects or academic specialties.

All this, however, speaks only to the question of whether humanities Ph.D.'s *can* find jobs outside of academe. Whether doctoral training in the humanities has value in such jobs is harder to assess. It can be argued that the training enhances general capabilities, an M.A. or Ph.D. giving added value to a liberal arts B.A. Training in law or in economics is thought somehow to provide advantages in business or government. The proposition is not farfetched on its face that literature, history, or philosophy can hone the mind at least as well as torts and real property, Phillips curves, or shadow prices. Alternatively, it can be argued that graduate training in a subject such as medieval literature, Latin American history, or phenomenology should be considered an indulgence, like a college tennis player's taking a fling on the tournament circuit or a college actor's working awhile in a repertory company— personally rewarding but in practical terms simply postponing progress in a career. It can even be contended that graduate training imposes a handicap. When a group of executives from the news media met with the two of us to discuss the subject matter of this book, nearly all said that they were disposed not to hire Ph.D.'s. A Ph.D., they agreed, was too little likely to be comfortable with the approximations of truth required by newspapers, newsmagazines, and radio and television. Executives in other industries similarly expressed doubt as to whether people who took years to write a dissertation could accommodate themselves to worldly deadlines.

Because of the great variety within the sample, the HERI survey results do not say clearly which of these hypotheses has the strongest empirical support. A distressingly high 54%

of the nonacademics rated themselves as underemployed, and only about a quarter of this group indicated that, for family or other reasons, they preferred to remain so. This group included not only the cabdrivers and tree trimmers but also a large number, mostly but not exclusively female, doing secretarial or clerical work—in most instances as employees of colleges or universities. Note should be taken, however, that the proportion rating themselves underemployed was not much smaller among teachers. In the faculty sample, 40% so described themselves. (See Table 3.1.)

The best evidence of how humanities Ph.D.'s appraise their training comes from the respondents' ratings of the extent to which particular skills or abilities had been enhanced by graduate training, coupled with their ratings of the importance of these skills or abilities in individual careers. Academics judged teaching ability and critical thinking to be far ahead of other

Table 3.1

Feelings of Underemployment among Humanities Graduate Alumni

	Percentages responding			
	Faculty	Academic adminis- trators	Other academic	Non- academic
Question: "Considering your ability, education, and experience, are you underemployed in your current position?"				
Yes; would prefer more challenging position	27	28	42	39
Yes; but for personal reasons prefer to remain in this or similar position	13	7	15	15
No	60	65	42	47
N	1571	169	122	813

needed skills, followed by a cluster that included general knowledge, insight, self-discipline, self-confidence, writing ability, and perseverance. Toward the bottom of their lists were research techniques, imagination, and leadership. Non-academics put critical thinking alone at the very top of their inventories. Self-confidence and self-discipline ranked high, followed by writing ability, perseverance, and general knowledge. Although the nonacademics tended to mention leadership more often than did the academics, they also placed it low, along with research techniques, imagination, and teaching ability. (See Tables 3.2 and 3.3.)

Reflecting on their graduate school experience, both groups concluded that it had enhanced more than anything else the

Table 3.2

Humanities Graduate Alumni's Evaluation of Skills and Abilities Enhanced by Graduate School

Item	Percentages responding "very much enhanced"			
	Faculty	Academic adminis-trators	Other academic	Non-academic
Critical thinking	81	82	77	78
Research techniques	81	87	81	76
Perseverance	68	78	63	58
Self-discipline	65	70	52	55
Insight	57	56	45	51
Writing ability	56	60	54	55
General knowledge	51	41	41	47
Cultural perspective	49	43	49	49
Self-confidence	48	48	37	41
Teaching ability	43	50	36	50
Imagination	28	25	23	29
Leadership ability	16	17	12	16
N	1439	157	113	778

Careers for Humanists

Table 3.3
Humanities Graduate Alumni's Estimates of Skills and Abilities
Important to Career

Item	Faculty	Academic adminis-trators	Other academic	Non-academic
		Percentages assigning item "very much" importance		
Critical thinking	91	94	83	84
Research techniques	64	45	70	53
Perseverance	73	81	72	69
Self-discipline	78	83	79	75
Insight	79	78	68	66
Writing ability	76	80	68	72
General knowledge	80	77	78	63
Cultural perspective	69	51	53	42
Self-confidence	76	91	70	76
Teaching ability	92	64	53	36
Imagination	62	61	48	52
Leadership ability	47	84	49	55
N	1409	154	138	759

one skill that both prized most highly—critical thinking. Many fewer than half of the academics thought it had equipped them with the other skill they valued—teaching ability. Both groups agreed that their other legacy was knowledge of research techniques, something to which fewer than two-thirds of the teachers and only a little more than half of the nonacademics attached great value. Among skills that both academics and nonacademics scored as important but of second order, self-discipline and perseverance were perceived by both as being helpful, followed by general knowledge and writing ability. Both groups agreed that graduate school had added little to their self-confidence, teaching ability, imagination, or capacity for leadership.

Though the humanities Ph.D.'s not in teaching careers cited fewer skills bettered by graduate school, their judgments and those of the academics were thus almost the same. Nonacademics generally believed their time in graduate school to have been well spent.

Thinking back on her own experience, Le Anne Schreiber said, "I have always believed that the process of analysis honed on anything works anywhere. . . . I believe that once a Ph.D. has a job outside he can see the usefulness of his training." Brawer said, "The logic you bring to doing good research is invaluable whether you're working on Chaucer or marketing lingerie . . . ." Evidence supporting his assertion is the fact that skills initially acquired for academe have carried him to a vice-presidency at Maidenform, Inc.

None of this evidence, of course, says whether former humanities graduate students not in academe are better off, as well off, or less well off than if, instead of studying literature or history, they had taken an LL.B. or an M.B.A. or simply started work straight out of college. William Persen, a Ph.D. in history who became vice-president of Business International in New York, argues that he has had a distinct advantage over others who had only the B.A. He had, he said, acquired the ability to use language with greater precision and "to see the multiplicity of choices in the world." He added, "You don't get that from undergraduate training." Anne Karalekas, another history Ph.D., worked for a U.S. Senate committee and then for a large consulting firm. She believes that her academic training has given her greater breadth of perspective than is characteristically found among either lawyers or M.B.A.'s. All that can be proven, however, is that men and women who do graduate work in the humanities and then go on to business or government do not regret their scholarly training, and do look back on it as having had lasting benefit.

As to whether such people enjoy work outside of academe, the answer is very clear. Many who initially hoped or expected to be college teachers found other occupations satisfying, and many who became teachers found their work *not* satisfying. On the whole, in fact, professors liked their jobs less than did humanities Ph.D.'s who were in administration or who were out editing magazines or marketing lingerie.

The disparity could, of course, be discounted as a function of academic melancholia. A closer look at what the two groups of respondents had to say provokes doubt, however, as to whether the differences can so easily be explained away.

Recipients of the questionnaire were asked to rate 18 aspects of their current jobs. In regard to 13 of these aspects, the teachers registered lower levels of satisfaction than did the nonacademics. They indicated significantly greater contentment only with their autonomy and independence, opportunity for scholarly pursuits, and opportunity for leisure. By wide margins, they rated lower than did nonacademics not only material aspects of their work—salary, fringe benefits, and opportunity for advancement—but also its social and psychological aspects. They were markedly less content regarding a sense of possessing responsibility or policymaking power. As compared with nonacademics, only about half as many academics indicated high satisfaction with the status of the institutions employing them. Perhaps most significant, they rated lower than did the nonacademics the challenge and variety of what they did, and they also rated lower the congeniality of their work relationships *and* the competence of their colleagues. (See Table 3.4.)

That those in academic life exhibited a relatively lower level of satisfaction on these last counts is hard to explain solely as a function of the academic temperament. Especially is this so because of contrasting evidence that the group of humanities Ph.D.'s most satisfied on most of these counts were those who remained in the academic environment as administrators. One

Table 3.4
Job Satisfaction among Humanities Graduate Alumni

	Percentages reporting themselves "very satisfied"			
Item	Faculty	Academic administrators	Other academic	Non-academic
Autonomy and independence	53	32	42	44
Variety in activities	36	35	40	42
Challenge	27	50	35	42
Congenial work relationships	37	53	40	41
Job security	37	40	30	40
Extent of responsibility	32	48	31	40
Status of employing institution/ organization	23	45	51	40
Fringe benefits	21	20	19	38
Working conditions (hours, location, etc.)	37	46	56	36
Status of position	34	45	23	32
Competence of colleagues	25	18	30	30
Salary	14	16	14	27
Career progress to date	21	35	23	26
Policymaking power	16	52	21	23
Opportunities for different (better) jobs at same institution/ organization	8	7	9	19
Opportunity for leisure time	21	9	18	17
Visibility for jobs at other institutions/ organizations	7	18	16	17
Opportunity for scholarly pursuits	22	9	18	17
N	1585	175	124	828

exception was competence of colleagues. The administrators were even more down on their peers than were the teachers. Although they felt a great deal less autonomous and independent and lamented their lack of leisure and opportunity for scholarship, academic administrators registered almost twice as much satisfaction with the challenge of their work. On most other counts they seemed more satisfied than faculty members.

That humanities Ph.D.'s should be comparatively less content as professors than as businesspersons or government officials or college presidents or deans is probably to be explained at least partly by evidence regarding attitudes of graduate students, for most students never considered any career except college teaching, and the majority had unrealistic notions about a professor's work life.

Asked to compare benefits of academic jobs with jobs in government or business, over 90% of humanities graduate students cited greater flexibility in the use of time. Two-thirds or more mentioned freedom to do as one wished, opportunities to experiment with differing life-styles, and ability to flout social conventions. On the down side, one-quarter to two-fifths expressed suspicion that a teaching job would carry less social prestige and less job security. They were divided almost evenly on whether teaching would involve less leisure or more. The chief drawback to the academic career identified by the majority was relatively lower earning power. (See Table 3.5.)

Interviews confirmed that most graduate students had little sense of the variety and complexity of the world outside academe. A doctoral candidate in philosophy at Stanford defined government work as "delivering mail." One in history at Berkeley said, "If you have morals or ideas, you can't last in government." A woman studying English at Bryn Mawr spoke of all corporations as populated by "little gray people." A woman at Berkeley in the same field defined a career in business as "being a waitress or a bottler of cough medicine for horses."

Table 3.5

Humanities Graduate Students' Perceptions of the Qualities of Academic and Nonacademic Careers[a]

Item	Percentages judging item present in academic life	
	Significantly less than in nonacademic life	Significantly more than in nonacademic life
Intellectual excitement	1	93
Cultural opportunities	1	90
Flexibility in use of time	3	89
Freedom to do what they wish	3	70
Opportunities to experiment with life-style	4	70
Ability to flout social conventions	6	58
Satisfaction in accomplishment	4	49
Leisure	29	35
Knowledge of human nature	13	34
Social prestige	27	27
Job security	43	17
Public influence	53	11
Earning power	84	3

[a] $N = 3992$.

Expressions of discontent by professors probably reflect disillusionment experienced upon learning what really lies on the other side of the podium. One graduate student interviewee voiced suspicion that his level of enthusiasm for Browning might fall by the time he had taught the poet's works five years in a row. One can infer from the survey data that many actually found this to be the case. Indeed, it is not hard to imagine experiences that could produce answers evidencing a low level of career satisfaction. Many college teachers find themselves repeating material that no longer excites them. Free time is swallowed in committee meetings (where doubts about the competence of colleagues develop and flourish) and in counseling sessions with students or parents. Experimentation with life-styles turns out to involve little more than a daily choice of whether to be costumed as a student or as a commuter. Meanwhile, the expected drawback does materialize. Whatever the life-style, it costs a lot. Much time and energy therefore go to lectures in extension courses or in summer school or to small-fee talks before local service clubs.

The survey results show clearly that dollars and cents turn out to be more important than most graduate students anticipate. To be sure, the students are right in supposing that certain academic environments can be rewarding in their own right. Among faculty members in the survey, those in universities were significantly more satisfied with their work than were those in 4-year colleges or 2-year colleges. They registered about the same levels of contentment as did administrators or people in business. (See Table 3.6.) But income was a factor, even for them. When those expressing generally high satisfaction with their work became specific, they cited satisfaction with expected earnings more often than any other factor. Nonacademics did so a little more frequently than academics but not much more so. The second factor that showed up most

Table 3.6

Job Satisfaction Reported by Humanities Graduate Alumni in Academic Employment, by Level of Institution

| | Percentages "very satisfied" | | |
Employer	Faculty	Academic administrators	Other academic
University	49	51	35
Four-year college	37	65	25
Two-year college	17	50	40

Humanists Outside Academe

Table 3.7

Earnings and Degree of Job Satisfaction Reported by Humanities Graduate Alumni, Academic and Nonacademic

Earnings	Percentages reporting high satisfaction			
	Faculty	Academic administrators	Other academic	Nonacademic
Below $10,000	31	—[a]	—[a]	27
$10,000–14,999	36	41	29	31
$15,000–19,999	45	45	52	45
$20,000–34,999	57	61	71	51
$35,000 or over	81	76	—[a]	67

[a] Fewer than 10 observations.

often was the extent to which the individual's job was related to his or her doctoral studies, though this held true only for academics.[4]

When scrutinized more closely, responses from the two groups actually turned out to be more different than at first appeared. With allowance made for all nuances, salary proved to be more than twice as important for nonacademics, whereas the relationship of job to doctoral study outstripped income as a determinant of satisfaction for academics. At comparable salaries, Ph.D.'s in teaching or academic administration tended to feel slightly more satisfied than nonacademics. Having a job related to doctoral study seemed to trade off with 12–15% of salary. Someone with earnings much more than 15% below the mean was prone to be dissatisfied, no matter how closely related the job. Someone with earnings 15% or more above the mean was likely to be comparatively satisfied with a job completely unrelated to his or her field of doctoral study. (See Tables 3.7 and 3.8.)

[4] In multiple regression calculations focusing on job satisfaction, the two most powerful explanatory variables were expected earnings, and relation of job to doctoral study. See Appendix, Table A.4.

Table 3.8

Earnings, Relationship of Job to Field of Doctoral Study, and Sense of Job Satisfaction among Humanities Graduate Alumni (percentages)

Job satisfaction	Relationship of job to doctoral study (by mean earnings)		
	Not at all	Somewhat	Closely related
Not satisfied	$11,971	$15,761	$16,488
Marginally satisfied	15,756	16,187	16,576
Satisfied	18,703	18,994	17,770
Very satisfied	23,448	22,843	20,244
N	482	595	1,482

That satisfaction levels for professors of humanities may be greatly influenced by salary level should cause no surprise. With their backs to the chalkboard, they are no longer in school; they are at work. The academic world becomes for them the "real world," with all its incentives and rewards. Though intellectual excitement and certain types of freedom may be easier to find in a college or university, and eccentricities of one variety or another may be more readily tolerated, the differences between academe and the rest of the world are marginal. The failure of graduate students to recognize the narrowness of the margin probably accounts for some of the dissatisfaction displayed by those who became teachers with little other work experience. It may also account for some of the high satisfaction felt by those who found the outside world more congenial than anticipated.

The principal findings from the survey of graduate alumni thus are, first, that those not in teaching careers regard their graduate education as enhancing skills they need and use in nonacademic work, and second, that, if paid well enough, they like what they do. Combined with other evidence, the dissatisfaction of many in teaching careers suggests that all people who are enthralled by literature, history, or philosophy are not necessarily people for whom teaching offers the most satisfying career. The remaining question is whether, even so, the ones who are cut out to be scholars have to be teachers if their scholarship is to thrive.

That scholarly writing can be done by people not employed as teachers is demonstrated by a few illustrious examples, most of whom are people who did not even need a Ph.D. Edmund Wilson, Barbara Tuchman, and Theodore White are three who had no occupation other than writing. Douglas Southall Freeman was a hardworking newspaper editor. Wallace Stevens was an insurance executive. Not many such examples jump to mind, to be sure, but neither does the mind instantly produce a long catalogue of professors comparable to such gifted and successful writers.

But it is not, in any case, works such as Wilson's *To the Finland Station* or Freeman's *Robert E. Lee* that are in question. Rather, it is the closely focused, carefully documented, not widely read article or monograph that provides the grist for syntheses such as Wilson's and Tuchman's. What is at issue is whether, for practical purposes, only people with professorships can or will produce such work.

In other countries it does occur. Sir Lewis Namier composed his meticulous histories of the parliaments of George III while working 10-hour days as secretary for a Zionist organization in London. Sir Harold Williams became one of the world's leading authorities on Swift while an active barrister and magistrate in the north of England. Montagu Woodhouse became a leading writer on modern Greek history while serving as a Conservative M.P., and Sergio Solmi and Antonello Gerbi acquired high standing among students of contemporary French literature and the history of Spain, respectively, while rising in the executive ranks of the Banca Commerciale of Milan. They have few counterparts in the United States.

It may be that this cannot change. Scholarship is facilitated and stimulated by contact with other scholars, including students in graduate seminars and undergraduate proseminars.

People who do not teach do not have this resource. The types of nonacademic jobs that provide satisfying challenge and variety are apt to make heavy demands on time and mental resources, and the person purposeful enough to have made a mark as a scholar is apt to be ambitious to succeed in a nonacademic environment and hence to devote most hours and thought to real-world problems rather than to texts or documents or theorems. And others do not have the professor's incentives. Their pay and status are not likely to improve as a result of publishing work on obscure, even arcane topics. More than in England or Europe, moreover, they may run risk of ridicule from co-workers or criticism from employers who feel that they should give their all to the jobs for which they are paid.

Survey and interview data demonstrate, however, that conditions outside the academic setting do not deter all people from pursuing scholarship. In the HERI sample of graduate alumni, the faculty group did more scholarly work than any other. Overall, faculty members were twice as likely as either academic administrators or nonacademics to have published a scholarly book or article. The striking fact, however, was the reciprocal. The average faculty member in the sample had published three-quarters of a scholarly book and just under three scholarly articles, whereas the average person in the nonacademic sample had published a third of a monograph and almost one and a half articles. (See Table 3.9.) Of course, some of the latter had previously been teachers and might have done their publishing while in academe. Even so, given a presumption that this was not true of all and that few people not employed as teachers could have expected to gain financially or otherwise, the fact that the amount of publication was so large suggests that some people not in academe are inwardly prompted to continue the activity for which they were trained in graduate school.

Also suggestive—though not encouraging—is evidence that academics in the sample did not derive much satisfaction from scholarly publication. About one-fifth of those who listed pub-

Table 3.9

Publications by Humanities Graduate Alumni, Academic and Nonacademic (mean numbers of publications)

	Faculty	Academic adminis- trators	Other academic	Non- academic
Scholarly books (single author)	.73	.30	.31	.32
Scholarly books (joint author)	.24	.22	.15	.18
Scholarly books (editor)	.47	.38	.55	.32
Chapters in scholarly books	.76	.55	.40	.40
Other books	.29	.30	.24	.39
Articles in scholarly journals	2.97	2.23	1.65	1.42
Other articles	1.28	1.54	1.28	1.51
Book reviews in scholarly journals	2.66	1.79	1.61	1.22

lications said they were very satisfied with their jobs, but when the entire pattern of answers was analyzed, what surfaced was an indication that this was the case because the record of scholarly publication correlated with income. For sheer satisfaction, independent of the money brought in, academics put nonscholarly publications far ahead. By a slight margin, nonacademics seemed to take more joy from scholarly work.[5] Perhaps it was because almost all of them did it simply because they wanted to.

Within the academic sample, wide differences appeared between those in universities, 4-year colleges, and 2-year col-

[5] In the regression calculations referred to in note 4, final betas correlating numbers of scholarly and nonscholarly publications with job satisfaction were, for academics, .029 and .072, with only the latter significant at the .05 level; for nonacademics, .072 and .020, with neither figure significant at that level. See Appendix, Table A.4.

leges. Faculty members in universities produced twice as many monographs and half again as many articles as did faculty members in 4-year colleges. (See Table 3.10.) Still, the more striking fact is that, person for person, graduate alumni not in teaching careers published more than did those teaching in 2-year colleges and almost as much as those teaching in 4-year colleges.

Once the fact is observed, the explanation seems obvious. The routine, repetitive, time-consuming, unexciting aspects of college teaching become more prominent the farther the remove from a research university. In a college not located near a major library, with only minimal library holdings of its own, a professor hired to be the one person "covering" a field faces forbidding obstacles even trying to be a teacher, let alone to be a scholar. In many such institutions, moreover, social pressures oppose scholarship. In nonacademic settings, the fact that an individual writes for learned journals represents no reproach to colleagues who have hobbies of a different sort.

Table 3.10
Publications by Humanities Faculty, by Level of Institution
(mean number of publications)

	University	4-year college	2-year college
Scholarly books (single author)	.84	.46	.24
Scholarly books (joint author)	.31	.16	.15
Scholarly books (editor)	.59	.25	.05
Chapters in scholarly books	.86	.43	.24
Other books	.33	.25	.13
Articles in scholarly journals	3.36	2.06	1.12
Other articles	1.45	1.36	.61
Book reviews in scholarly journals	2.85	1.94	.95

In a college, it may be otherwise. Commenting on his own impressive publication record, a professor of philosophy from a small school in the Midwest observed that in his environment "such activities were neither encouraged nor rewarded. The sole incentive was internal."

That a person with such internal motivation can find a non-academic environment congenial is suggested by the example of James Cortada. He did not make a choice between a life in scholarship and one in business. Instead, he developed a captain's paradise. When a graduate student in history, he recognized that his passion for reconstructing nineteenth-century Spain made him too much an antiquarian to reach the very top of the academic tree. Making an early decision not to teach, he finished up a Ph.D. in 3 years and cultivated his quantitative talents. After graduate school he went to work selling computers for IBM. He did so with a conviction that IBM's latest models in fact represented the best that a customer could buy. Earning a large income and controlling his time, he was able to order first editions from Spanish booksellers and to take time off to visit archives. By his early thirties, he had a list of articles and books, in both Spanish and English, long enough to inspire envy in a full professor twice his age.[6] "I like the realism of business," he said. "I like having known benchmarks. In business I use history and the skills I developed in graduate study. I also have freedom. . . . I never had the academic ideal of the integration of my life and work. That's part of the academic myth."

Within James Cortada is an inner fire. He would have done what he did almost regardless of how he earned his living. Most humanities Ph.D.'s are not thus driven. Many who became productive scholars as professors might not have

---

[6] James Cortada's most recent historical works are *Two Nations over Time: Spain and the United States, 1776–1977* (Westport, Conn.: Greenwood Press, 1978) and *Spain in the Twentieth Century World* (Westport, Conn.: Greenwood Press, 1980). Their bibliographies provide leads to his other writings.

done so had they taken other jobs. Although it is clear that people other than professors can produce scholarship, it is equally clear that their doing so requires considerable extra effort. We must therefore turn next to the question of whether it is feasible to lighten that requirement—to make scholarly research and writing easier for people who have the necessary training but who by either necessity or choice earn their living in jobs other than teaching.

4

What Is to Be Done

During the 1970s, such gatherings of humanists as the annual meetings of the Modern Language Association (MLA), the American Historical Association (AHA), and the American Philosophical Association (APA) were dominated by the discussion of the question of what was to happen to Ph.D.'s who could not find jobs as teachers. As the previous chapter suggests, there seems to be an answer to that question. They have gotten and will get other types of jobs. Most will enjoy their work as much as they would have enjoyed teaching. Very few face actual unemployment. Judging from survey data, the proportion believing themselves underemployed will be similar to that among the Ph.D.'s who did find teaching jobs. (See Table 3.1.) To be sure, tens of thousands of doctoral students and Ph.D.'s will have experienced pain, disappointment, and dislocation. In most cases, however, their personal trials will turn out to have been brief, and the majority will look back on their years in graduate school as having been not badly spent.

The harder question is this: What is to happen to the humanities? What is truly uncertain about the decades ahead is whether there will continue to be a flow of articles and books enlarging and deepening understanding of literature, history, and philosophy.

It can be argued, to be sure, that a depression in the academic labor market, even if prolonged and severe, will not seriously affect the quantity or quality of scholarly research and writing. This argument cannot be dismissed out of hand, for it is a fact that the majority of people with doctoral training have not and do not function as scholars. An early 1970s survey of college teachers in the humanities found that fewer than half had produced a book, and only about 1 out of 7 had written more than 2 books. Almost half had never even published an article. A survey of the late 1970s found only a third of humanities teachers with no scholarly publications to their credit but also not much more than a third entitled to be described as productive scholars. (See Table 4.1.)

In the 1930s, the entire pool of people in the United States with scholarly training in the humanities amounted to only a few thousand, yet that decade is generally considered a very creative period in humanistic scholarship. Certainly, it was a fruitful period. The *American Historical Review* was publishing each quarter-year reviews of more than 30 new books by

Table 4.1
Publications by College Teachers of Humanities (percentages)

Publications	1972–1973	1976–1977
Articles		
None	49	33
1–2	19	21
3–4	11	12
5 or more	21	34
Books		
None	59	n.a.
1–2	26	n.a.
3 or more	14	n.a.

Sources: Alan E. Bayer, *Teaching Faculty in Academe, 1972–73*, American Council on Education Research Reports, No. 2 (1973), and unpublished analyses of the same data prepared by Bayer for the Higher Education Research Institute; *Chronicle of Higher Education*, 28 November 1977, p. 8.

American scholars. The *American Bibliography* of the Modern Language Association, listing both books and articles by American scholars, averaged 1710 items a year.

It obviously did not require tens of thousands of scholars to keep the humanities in good health. Indeed, one can go on to note that fifth-century Athens did fairly well with a total population below that of present-day Scranton or Cedar Rapids. The total number of humanists may have no more bearing on the vitality of the humanities than the number of composers and painters has on the vitality of music and art.

Since even the most pessimistic projections envision several thousand career openings on college faculties, there may be no cause for concern about humanistic scholarship. True scholars may know their vocation. Those destined to shape knowledge may obtain the training they need, undeterred by awareness that professorships will be few. After all, people who became scholars in the 1930s faced a scarcity of teaching jobs and, on top of that, the fact that salary levels were still based on an assumption that professors had independent means. Because the 1960s and 1970s saw the upgrading of so many colleges and universities, teaching posts suitable for dedicated scholars are now actually far more numerous than in the 1930s. For reasons outlined in Chapter 1, these posts will probably be filled, regardless of what happens in the rest of the academic labor markets. Scholarly research and publication could thus proceed, largely unaffected by a general depression in higher education.

There are, however, reasons for doubting that, in this respect, the 1980s and 1990s will be analogous to the 1930s. To begin with, it seems possible that relatively fewer talented and ambitious people will seek training. In the 1930s conditions were bad everywhere. Many people saw the alternative to graduate school and a teaching job as no job at all. In the time ahead, most are apt to see their choice as between competing for professorships that are few or poorly paid or both and, on the other hand, entering some profession where opportunities are multiplying and levels of compensation are rising. Humanities B.A.'s of the 1980s and 1990s could easily conclude that their vocations are in law or public policy or business administration. As indicated earlier, survey data suggest that the proportion of purposeful, career-oriented graduate students may already have declined. (See pp. 46–50.)

A second question is whether people who do go to graduate school will get the training they need if they are to succeed as scholars. As was also pointed out earlier, many students base their choices on short-term economic considerations. They go where paid teaching assistantships are available. The institutions having the most funds for this purpose are not necessarily those best equipped to train scholars. With only a handful of institutions offering doctoral training in the 1930s, would-be scholars had few opportunities to make mistakes. Those of the 1980s and 1990s will face strong temptation to disperse themselves among universities, many of which lack faculty strength or research facilities that most apprentices need if they are to master the scholar's craft. Such an outcome is all the more likely in view of the fact that the strongest research universities have nearly all responded to the prospective shortfall in academic jobs by slicing back admissions to doctoral programs.

Third, people who do enroll in well-equipped graduate departments may drop out before they have sufficient training. With the completion of a doctorate taking on the average 2 years longer than in the 1930s or the 1950s, even dedicated and ambitious students could decide that they should be in a professional school or out in the world. Surrounded by advanced graduate students and junior faculty nervous about job prospects, many students could give up without completing even rudimentary training.

Finally, it is possible that the Ph.D.'s or near-Ph.D.'s with greatest promise as scholars may not be the ones selected by the colleges and universities best outfitted for scholarship. To be sure, almost all Ph.D.'s are likely to be able to teach. Even if career openings are few, short-term openings are sure to be abundant. If one-quarter of faculty posts are without tenure and are occupied by one person for only 3–4 years on the average, then several thousand posts will become vacant every year. As remarked earlier, however, large numbers of these teaching posts will not be suited to would-be scholars.

Posts that do offer opportunity for scholarly work may not match the scholars available to fill them, for universities and colleges usually hire people to fill instructional needs. Within any 2- to 4-year period, the schools most hospitable to scholarship may have no openings at all in many of the scores of specialties into which the humanities in practice subdivide. The distribution of quality in a given period's crop of Ph.D.'s in modern languages, for example, might be heavily skewed toward Slavic literatures. In the same period, the best colleges and universities might have vacancies only for teachers of Romance tongues. The Slavicists might be shunted into places discouraging for scholarly work, and at some point even the most dedicated scholars might decide to go into a different line of work.

Even if they have appropriate slots, colleges and universities hospitable to research may not pick the people best able to contribute to scholarship. They do not have very reliable criteria for judging scholarly promise. In the humanities, distinguished work requires both depth of original research and reflectiveness. A doctoral dissertation or even a first book seldom serves as a sure indication of the subsequent accomplishments of any critic, historian, or philosopher. Thus, even if adequate numbers of talented people seek and obtain training for scholarship, the academic appointment process could frustrate hopes that the humanities will survive in good health through a long period in which attractive career openings in higher education become fewer.

It follows that some special effort may be required if the 1980s and 1990s are not to be a period in which humanistic scholarship languishes. To specify possible lines of effort, however, is exceptionally difficult. It is probably idle to conjure up notions that call for new outlays of money, whether from public or from private sources. In addition, there exist no readily identifiable organizations or agencies to which recommendations for action might be presented.

The first of these problems needs to be stressed, for panels on the "academic job crisis" at humanists' conventions often feature an argument that the problem would disappear if the nation had its priorities in the right order. It is customarily pointed out that the federal government's annual outlays for defense have shot above $200 billion. If 1% or even a fraction of 1% of that money were used to fund humanistic research, runs the argument, practically all current and prospective Ph.D.'s in the humanities could put their training to work. Though this contention elicits nods and handclaps, it cannot be said to embody much realism. The Armed Services committees and the defense subcommittees of the Appropriations committees of the House and Senate do not authorize money for research in the humanities. The Human Resources and Education and Labor committees and their associated appropriations subcommittees do. Even if not in a mood to retrench on all fronts, these bodies would look at proposals to underwrite employment of humanities Ph.D.'s as in competition with aid to dependent children, elementary and secondary education, equal employment opportunity efforts, and the like. Similar conditions exist at state and city levels. It is probably in vain to hope that public outlays for the humanities will even remain at the levels of the 1970s, let alone be increased by a margin sufficient to promise a secure future for humanistic scholarship.

What holds for public funds probably holds equally for those of universities and private foundations. The revenues of universities have hitherto been the chief source of support for scholarship in literature, history, and philosophy. In an era of declining enrollments, these resources will shrink. Even though, as pointed out earlier, funds need not go down in proportion to enrollments, allocations for graduate education, faculty research, and scholarly publication are particularly vulnerable. It is hard to imagine an institution where discretionary money could go to research travel or even to library acquisitions at the expense of maintaining real wage levels for tenured faculty and administrators.

As for private foundations, they reduced outlays on the humanities during the 1970s. New legislation curbed what they could do. Inflation meanwhile lessened their resources, and claims upon them multiplied. Even in the cultural area, petitions for support of scholarship came to compete with appeals for the maintenance of symphonies, opera companies, and galleries. Were foundation contributions to the humanities to inch up during the 1980s and 1990s, that would be the most that could be expected.

Any hardheaded approach ought thus to assume almost no new money from any source. It should ask only transfers of resources, the total amount of which could well be diminishing rather than growing.

The second obstacle may also need more ample description, for panelists discussing the "academic job crisis" are also prone to call upon their professional associations for remedial action. In fact the MLA, AHA, and APA are powerless bodies. They are not at all analogous to the American Bar Association or the American Medical Association. Though their annual meetings can adopt resolutions, those resolutions are even less enforceable than planks in a party platform. The American Association of University Professors (AAUP) is for practical purposes a collective bargaining agent for certain college teachers who already have jobs. The Association of American Universities, the American Association for Higher Education, and other such organizations of college and university administrators exist chiefly for exchange of information. Each such organization can serve as a forum for the discussion of various approaches to protecting the future of humanities scholarship. In the end, however, any approach that succeeds will have to be one entailing independent, largely uncoordinated moves by large numbers of individuals and organizations.

Even so, the prospect may not be hopeless. The question is whether current resources could be shifted about to ensure (*a*) that sufficient numbers of able young people obtain advanced training in humanistic scholarship and (*b*) that those so equipped and motivated be able to do research and to publish the results. Many people would like to see these things happen. Almost no one would oppose them. Something may therefore occur if interested parties merely make the right choices among alternative ways of doing what they already want to do.

With regard to the first hazard—that the numbers of talented people seeking scholarly training may fall off—the obvious remedy is not, in any case, to spend more money. Rather, it is to alter attitudes. The pool of potential trainees will remain large, for even "worst-case" assumptions yield projections of humanities B.A.'s running well over 50,000 a year with perhaps 15,000–20,000 enrolling in graduate school. (See Table 2.2.)

The nation's universities have ample capacity to train scholars in these or even larger numbers, and they need no new resources for the purpose. Prior to the 1960s, 25 universities trained two-thirds of humanities Ph.D.'s. By the mid-1970s, the top 25 were turning out less than 40%, and the top 40 accounted for not quite 60%. (See Table 2.11.) Not all of these 40 had strong departments in all the humanities. On the other hand, some schools not among the 40 offered training equal to the best. Princeton and Bryn Mawr are examples. There can be almost no question that the United States has graduate departments in the humanities able to accommodate any B.A.'s interested in a crack at scholarly training.

And it is probably the case that universities could train graduate students in such numbers with little or no strain on their budgets, perhaps even with some net financial gain. Since graduate seminars are small and doctoral candidates receive a great deal of individual instruction, on the surface graduate education seems to be an expensive business. If a professor spends half of his or her classroom time on a large group of undergraduates and the other half on a small group of graduate students, simple arithmetic suggests that the university's per-student costs are much higher for the second group.

This is, however, an illusion. In the first place, the professor's time is not perfectly transferable. The replacement for the small group of graduate students would probably not be a second large group of undergraduates. It might be a small group of undergraduates. It might equally well be an equivalent number of hours simply doing research, for the university professor whose specialty is Goethe or medieval economic life or the philosophy of Heidegger is likely to have a limited repertoire of courses, many with less than universal appeal to undergraduates.

In the second place, for professors, the training of graduate students is often only in part a teaching activity. In small or large part, it is likely to overlap with research and scholarly writing. Students in a graduate seminar often pursue aspects of a subject on which their professor is doing research. Sometimes they are, for all practical purposes, research assistants paid with course credit rather than money. Sometimes—in the very best seminars—students and professors are collaborators. Even though some of the doyens of humanistic scholarship are at Princeton's Institute for Advanced Study, which has no students, one may argue that many scholars do better work as scholars because they train graduate students. It is even arguable that, if universities see their function as partly the advancement of learning, they need critical masses of graduate students both for the stimulation of their current faculty and for its ultimate replenishment. If these universities do not have graduate students, in other words, they would have cause to try to create them.

In the third place, graduate students form a large pool of cheap labor. The AAUP has estimated that top-level universities would have to enlarge their faculties by 25% if they tried to maintain existing student–teacher ratios without using graduate teaching assistants.[1] These assistants make it possible for universities to give undergraduates both exposure to a significant proportion of their leading scholars and the intimacy of small-group discussion. Universities thus derive positive benefits from having comparatively large numbers of graduate students.

Conditions vary, of course, from university to university. In those with few or no undergraduates, such as the University of Chicago and the Graduate Center of the City University of New York (CUNY), having a graduate student population clearly involves some net costs. At an institution with many thousands of undergraduates, such as Ohio State, the ability to use graduate students for undergraduate teaching involves substantial net savings. For most universities, it is probably the case that a true balance sheet would have the corps of graduate students in the assets column.

The market pricing of graduate instruction already reflects these realities. Fees usually appear to be set at levels equal to or above those for undergraduate instruction. This blocks outcries from parents of undergraduates and alumni. It also enables universities to get as much money as possible out of government agencies and foundations that award graduate scholarships. In reality, much of the apparent revenue is rebated in the form of university scholarships and research or teaching stipends. Universities thus get graduate teaching assistants even more cheaply, for part of what they appear to pay them is merely a credit offsetting their own charges. In practice, graduate training itself has been virtually a free good, the costs to universities having been largely a result of competition in offering fellowship stipends over and above tuition.

[1] *Academe*, vol. 11, no. 4 (December 1977).

There is no obvious reason why the basic condition need change. In all probability, universities could, without financial penalty, continue in the 1980s and 1990s to train about as many humanities graduate students as in the 1960s and 1970s.

What threatens the inflow of qualified trainees is neither a shortage of potential students nor the costs of providing training; it is the widespread assumption that the only function of the training is to prepare people for lifetime careers in college teaching. It is this assumption, combined with warnings about academic job prospects, that causes college graduates, intellectually excited by poetry or history or philosophy and motivated to explore frontiers in the humanities, regretfully to apply to law schools or business schools and to forgo training for scholarship. It is precisely the same assumption that leads the major graduate departments to curtail admissions, turning away even people who say that they are not concerned by the fact that their training may not lead directly to employment.

If the numbers of well-qualified entrants to graduate programs are not to decline sharply in decades ahead, the basic assumption has to change. At least to some extent, the evidence presented in earlier chapters should be sufficient to shake it. The survey data show, on the one hand, that interest in graduate training in the humanities is not chiefly a function of desire to teach. The fact that graduate students see elementary and secondary teaching as no more attractive than a career in business indicates their general attitude. (See Table 4.2.) Among students whom we interviewed, not more than a third exhibited enthusiasm for year-in, year-out classroom teaching of basic subjects—even subjects such as Shakespeare or Plato. Though almost all graduate students said they wanted to teach in a 4-year college or university, what those in the interview groups talked about longingly was the seminar or discussion group in which all participants were engaged in a process of discovery.

The survey data also show that, although graduate training is an asset for people who become teachers, it is equally an

Table 4.2
Humanities Graduate Students' Perceptions of Teaching and Nonteaching Careers[a]

Career	Percentages rating career "very unattractive"	Percentages rating career "very attractive"
Teaching		
Four-year college	3	93
Two-year college	25	46
Elementary or secondary school[b]	64	14
Business training	78	9
Research		
Academic setting	19	62
Nonprofit agency[b]	48	32
Business setting	77	9
Administration		
College or university	59	19
Elementary or secondary school[b]	54	24

Business (executive or supervisory)	71	13
Government service	59[c]	21[c]
VISTA, Peace Corps, etc.	64	15
Other, in own field	42	38
Other, not related to doctoral field	72	10
Military	91	4
Other	46	33
Communications media (TV, publishing, etc.)[a]	21	55
Professional library work	70	12

[a] N = 3778.

[b] On the questionnaire, teaching and administration at the elementary or secondary level formed a single option; the same was true of research and administration in a nonprofit agency. For employment in communications media, the questionnaire did not specify type of employment.

[c] Excluding military service; the figures are 67 and 17, if it is included.

asset for those who pursue other careers. Those who do teach do not see the experience as having improved their ability to teach. Teachers and nonteachers alike see it as having enhanced critical thinking and ability to do research, the latter something almost as prized outside academe as within it. (See Tables 3.2 and 3.3.)

There thus exists some basis for saying the following to graduating college seniors:

> If you want to do graduate work in the humanities, your reason is probably interest in the subject rather than a well-considered inclination to pursue a career in college teaching.
>
> Graduate training will sharpen your critical faculties, give you some research skills, and perhaps equip you to do some scholarly writing. It could open up to you the possibility of a spell as a college teacher, conceivably even a lifetime in that occupation, and you cannot otherwise add that option to your string.
>
> But you should not enroll in graduate school on the assumption that teaching in college is even what you will *want* to do, let alone what you *will* do.
>
> If you end up in a line of work where an advanced degree in humanities is not a job qualification, the opportunity cost of your time in graduate school will obviously not have been zero. On the other hand, it will not necessarily turn out to have been high. Although your pay and status may at first be lower than if you had gone to work sooner, there is a good chance that in the long run you will do a better job and be better compensated by virtue of the finer tuning of your critical faculties and research talents.
>
> So think chiefly about whether you want graduate training for its own sake rather than for the sake of the job for which it might qualify you. Reckon the costs, including the possible opportunity costs, and make your decision accordingly.

If graduate departments could become comfortable about saying something of this sort to would-be applicants, their own inhibitions about admitting new students ought to relax. Their admissions quotas could then become functions not of professors' consciences, abetted by pressures from incumbent graduate students, but of the applicant pool, their own training capabilities, and their particular system for pricing graduate instruction.

Although realistic advice to graduating seniors, coupled with changes in the admissions policies of key graduate departments, would improve chances for recruiting scholarly talent, some other changes may be necessary complements. A senior aged 22 might reasonably conclude that, as a business executive of 40, he or she would be better off and more satisfied with life if 2 of the intervening 18 years had been spent in graduate school instead of on the job. Contemplation of a doctoral program with a median duration of 7 years, however, could well lead to an opposite conclusion.

It follows that universities desiring to recruit humanities doctoral candidates should develop programs enabling students to move into nonteaching careers with a minimum of lost time and effort. The New York State Regents "Careers in Business" program pioneered at NYU, mentioned earlier, provided a 7-week cram course that enabled carefully selected Ph.D.'s and near-Ph.D.'s to move into jobs at levels of salary and responsibility well above those for people with B.A.'s alone. Other universities adopted the NYU model. For the most part, these programs served to facilitate career change by people who had completed Ph.D.'s and spent some time as college teachers, but concluded that they preferred different types of challenges. The short summer course offering orientation to business or government is, however, a device that universities could well borrow as an add-on to 1- or 2-year master's degree programs. Potentially self-financing, it could be an actual source of revenue to universities.

Another possible device is a master's program combining initial training in scholarship with training for a profession. A multiyear curriculum could lead to simultaneous award of an M.A., M.Phil., or M.Litt. in a humanities discipline and an LL.B., or J.D., or M.B.A. or even M.D. Though entailing interfaculty negotiations and some redefinition by humanities departments of the requirements for initiation into scholarship, such programs could attract potential scholars who would otherwise never acquire the rudiments of training or test their talent for research and writing.

A third variant could be introductory training in scholarship coupled with formal, tested practice in concise writing, clear oral exposition, and guidance of small groups—skills associated with teaching but equally useful for and prized in other occupations. For such programs, universities in large cities could almost certainly draw at relatively little cost on alumni or others professionally engaged in providing comparable types of training in corporations or government agencies, thus providing some genuine capability for certifying acquisition of general capabilities beyond those of a B.A.

These suggestions are merely illustrative. Many possibilities exist. Since charges for graduate study are already artificial, one other line of experimentation could involve additional tinkering with prices. For example, course fees could be set at attractively low levels with most real or apparent charges being levied only when and if a degree is awarded. Yet another possibility, perhaps too radical even to be suggested, is for major graduate departments to schedule some courses and seminars for weekends for the convenience of part-time students who have full-time jobs.

What is appropriate or feasible may differ from university to university, even from department to department. The critical shift required is one of attitude—toward the view that the aim of graduate education is to train people interested in scholarship, not to feed a particular labor market. If that shift occurs, the rest is mere adaptation.

With regard to the character of the training offered as distinct from recruitment into training programs, a separate set of issues exists. Traditionally, humanities doctoral programs have had three components. Featuring seminar papers and a culminating dissertation, preparation for research has been the most prominent. The acquisition of broad knowledge has come second, oriented to a qualifying examination—usually the daunting "doctor's oral"—presumably because of student need to be able to define research topics *and* to teach. The third component, seldom required and sometimes dispensed with, has been practice teaching.

The new circumstances do not demand changes. Research training is the heart of any doctoral program, and both seminars and dissertations seem necessary. When University of Michigan Ph.D.'s were polled in 1974–1975, only a handful, whether in academic or nonacademic jobs, questioned the usefulness of their dissertation work.[2] Qualifying examinations would probably be much the same if designed for students who did not expect to teach. And practice teaching serves not only to finance graduate training but also to supply experience that may be directly useful in other settings. In any case, any group of students is sure to include some who will spend some portion of their lives as teachers.

New questions concerning the training of humanists have to do less with basic elements than with duration and intensity. It has always been the case that people could take Ph.D.'s and prepare for nonteaching careers. They simply added 2–5 years in professional schools. If students in the future were encouraged to combine Ph.D.'s and professional degrees, Ph.D. programs would have to be altered, for almost any of the possible formulas would require some interruption in the constant several-year-long master–apprentice relationship heretofore characteristic. And none would attract ambitious and purposeful students unless both degrees could be completed within some reasonable period. A department in which the median time for the Ph.D. alone remained 7 years would probably draw few such students, no matter what its distinction or strength.

Another question concerning future doctoral training has to do with selectivity after admission. The alternatives can be

---

[2] "The Role of the Dissertation in Doctoral Education at the University of Michigan," mimeographed, Horace H. Rackham School of Graduate Studies (July 1976).

characterized as the funnel versus the cylinder. The first figure implies admission of a large number of novices but progressive elimination of those judged weak, with only a small number ending up as Ph.D.'s. The second figure implies the opposite: a complete course of training for as many as possible of those originally admitted. In between the extremes are many combinations. One argument for the funnel is that, if openings in college teaching do diminish significantly, the supply of Ph.D.'s would come closer to academic market demand. A second is that it permits concentration of faculty time on the students who seem most promising. For the contrary model, the primary argument is that judgments on the promise of graduate students are uncertain and apt to be wrong. A secondary argument is that a number of subfields need scholarly tending, even if by people whose own minds are not extraordinarily creative or original.

The issue can be further complicated by introducing the question of whether selectivity should have to do with continuation in course or simply with allocation of support. Should a paying customer be able to stay on almost regardless of other factors? Should teaching assistantships be awarded on the basis of scholarly promise or probable teaching proficiency?

The questions are ones likely to be answered differently in different institutions. The model of the funnel is apt to attract the elite institutions; the model of the cylinder, the institutions with most need for new graduate teaching assistants. If so, the result could be that many Ph.D.'s of the 1980s and 1990s will hold degrees from the latter. If this likelihood sparks concern in the elite schools, some of them might adopt a variant resembling—to stretch the metaphor—a funnel with a bubble or retort below the point. They could, for example, develop examinations on the basis of which they would admit for dissertation research some students who had taken basic graduate training elsewhere.

The greater the variety of opportunities, the larger should be the number of people finding that they have a bent for humanistic scholarship and going on to acquire the knowledge and skills needed for producing scholarly work. Since the median time for a Ph.D. is never likely to drop below 5 years, it may be especially important that those students who reveal the greatest scholarly promise—those who might make the best use of doctoral training—do not see completion of a Ph.D. as necessarily committing them to competition for a restricted set of professorships. For them, "Careers in Business" programs and other such transition aids may have particular value in that their very existence provides reassurance that other doors are not necessarily closed. Since some of the most successful products of these programs are people who changed occupation after several years on college faculties, appearances by such alumni and alumnae at functions of graduate departments could reinforce the effect.

In order to increase the chances that promising students complete their training and then actually produce scholarly work, it is even more important that opportunities plainly exist for the pursuit of scholarship by people who happen not to be professors. It is undoubtedly romantic to suppose that a very large fraction of significant scholarship will ever come from people dependent on salaries from institutions other than colleges, universities, or research centers. It is probably not unrealistic, however, to suppose that the fraction could be larger than it is at present and that, in a long period when teaching posts are scarce or poorly paid or both, the fraction could be substantial.

As matters stand, scholars who are not professors suffer severe handicaps. In most cases, they do not have schedules as flexible as those of people whose only fixed commitments are in classrooms. The disadvantage is made much greater when libraries, archives, and museums cope with financial pressures by curtailing hours or privileges with concern chiefly for their student and teacher customers. Would-be scholars with nine-to-five jobs can only use research facilities open at nights and on weekends.

Scholars not in academe are likely to be isolated. They lack opportunities to discuss their ideas or findings with people who share their interests and knowledge. To be sure, many scholars on college faculties are also isolated, either because of their colleges or because of their colleagues. As a rule, however, they at least have entrée to learned societies, where a little effort can bring into being a panel at a regional or national association meeting. Scholars whose stationery carries only a home address or the emblem of a corporation or an operating government agency can do likewise only with great effort, more than likely involving an exercise of influence by some intermediary in or near academe.

Few scholars not associated with colleges or universities have any incentive to publish. Exception has to be made, of course, for official government historians, curators of historical societies and museums, and others who have lately begun to style themselves "public historians." Exception also has to be made for the tiny number, symbolized by Barbara Tuchman, capable of producing best-sellers. For the majority, the only reason for putting something in print is either private vanity or an almost fanatical belief in the importance of some finding or findings.

At least equal must be the number of people tempted to prepare a scholarly article or monograph but put off by fear of ridicule. One source of such fear lies among nonacademic friends, associates, or relatives: "You wouldn't believe how Dolores spends *her* weekends." Another source lies among the in-group of academics dominating learned journals and scholarly publishing houses: "Our reviewers feel that your manuscript shows insufficient familiarity with recent changes in interpretation initiated by Professor X."

Over the next few decades, humanistic scholarship will have a much better chance of thriving if, in addition to nourishing the flow of apprentice scholars, graduate deans and departments and interested foundation and government officials were to exert some effort to lower the obstacles that currently block research and publication by scholars not in academic institutions.

The first specific measure is profoundly needed, even if humanistic scholarship is exclusively the product of university people or even if the output of such scholarship should temporarily dwindle or cease. It is the maintenance of facilities for research—in particular the Library of Congress and the nation's major university libraries. All scholarly libraries are in trouble, for prices of books have soared, and costs for cataloguing, holding, and circulating them have gone up yet more. Even the Library of Congress has been forced to make economies. The New York Public Library has practically been compelled to cease adding to its collections and to cut to a minimum its services to scholars. The nation's other great repositories are in stages of invalidism bracketed between these extremes.

Here, a case can be made for spending more money, not just making transfers. The Library of Congress and a dozen or so state, state university, and private university libraries are national treasures. Their collections need to be maintained for the sake of future generations. If humanistic scholarship languishes in the last decades of the twentieth century, that will be a misfortune. If the major libraries develop serious gaps in their collections, that will be a calamity. It might prove irreparable.

In connection with humanistic scholarship as a whole, the temptation occasionally arises to argue that it may serve some unsuspected national need. Had the United States had scholars who understood Vietnamese history and civilization, runs a recent version, the American people might have been spared a grim and humiliating war. Thus put, the argument is overblown, perhaps meretricious. It resembles the case for space exploration based on the incidental discovery of Teflon. On the other hand, the thesis that the United States should have on hand collections of research materials relating to a wide range of problems, domestic as well as foreign, that might arise over the centuries ahead is surely one that deserves respect and that ought to influence both government appropriations and the outlays of foundations.

With regard to scholars as distinct from materials for scholarship, the question is how to improve conditions for nonacademic scholars without additional money, perhaps even in circumstances in which money now going to scholars goes instead to libraries.

The first problem is how to ensure that scholars not employed as teachers are able to do research. They must be able to use libraries and archives, and this means that hours of access have to include at least some evenings and weekends. Since professors and students do have somewhat more flexible hours, they should be able to adjust without great difficulty to slight shifts in library and archive schedules—say to a 10:00 A.M. or even a noon opening time. Alternatively, some facilities might offer after-hours services to people paying special annual users' fees that cover the extra costs. The scholar not in academe is in need of consideration but not necessarily of charity.

The intellectual isolation of scholars not in academe could be eased if they had opportunities for more free and frequent interchange with those who are associated with universities, for universities will continue to be almost the only places with congregations of people sharing strong interest in particular fields of literature, history, or philosophy. Such opportunities are unlikely to arise spontaneously. On their own initiative, few professors are apt to hunt up scholars who are outside academic circles, and few nonacademics will push themselves on professors.

If change is to occur, it will have to be brought about chiefly by university administrators. One reason for their doing so resides in the fact that the nonacademics represent a potential reserve of cheap labor. The common impulses of administrators and professors have already created a large group of second-class academics employed part-time and/or at low wages to teach English composition, introductory language, and other subjects that few professors like to teach. This group could well expand, especially in universities that engineer or experience reduction in numbers of graduate students.

In the future, however, administrators and professors could unite to produce something healthier. Even though their enrollments will not drop, major universities are likely to show some response to financial pressures. Some professors who die or retire will not be replaced. They are most likely to be ones teaching esoteric subjects. The specialist on the twentieth-century United States will have a successor; the specialist on the history of Brazil may not.

In some instances a partial remedy could be an adjunct appointment. A Ph.D. specializing in Brazilian history who keeps up with the field but who happens to work for a bank could give a once-a-week evening course or seminar for interested students. He or she would enjoy it and would probably ask minimal compensation. If satisfied with the individual's quality and sure that in fact nothing more could be had, the department could at least feel that it was maintaining the field. The president or dean could take comfort in not sacrificing all academic variety for the sake of economy. Though the numbers would probably not be large, they might be sufficient both to set before undergraduates role models of scholars not in academe and to catalyze interchange between scholars employed as teachers and those not so employed.

As for the professional associations, one can probably count on nonteaching scholars proving able on their own to gain adequate entrée. During the late 1970s, they came more and more into evidence, partly because people hoping for academic jobs arranged to be included on programs but partly also because members concerned about the "academic job crisis" formed effective committees. Unfortunately, the associations' annual meetings seem likely to serve less and less well as showcases for scholarly work, whether that of academics or nonacademics, for inflationary increases in travel and hotel costs have greatly curtailed attendance by people other than those interviewing or being interviewed to fill academic jobs. Local, regional, or other meetings may increasingly serve as substitutes.

Even if library and archive schedules remain unchanged and universities continue to shut out all who are not their own and the learned societies either wither or serve primarily groups of professors, it is arguable that scholarly research and writing could still be done by people outside academe if they have some continuing incentives. The key question thus is whether something could be done to create such incentives.

The obstacles are many. In current practice, financial support for humanistic research most often takes the form of paid leaves of absence for professors. Sabbatical leaves provided by colleges and universities from their own resources are supplemented by fellowship awards from the Guggenheim Foundation, the American Council of Learned Societies, the National Endowment for the Humanities, and other private and public sources.

Steady, perhaps precipitate, diminution in the amount of money available to underwrite humanistic scholarship seems almost inevitable. Universities will be pinched and, as already noted, will be under pressure to transfer funds to their libraries. Public agencies will probably have to spread their largesse more and more thinly. Foundations may well do likewise. The most likely prospect is a shrinking total, with individual awards or subsidies becoming more meager.

At the same time, the financial needs of scholars promise to increase. With heavier workloads or declining pay or both, those in academe will be less and less able to arrange for or finance free time, research travel, and the like. Except for people who secure for themselves the freedom and income of a Jim Cortada, scholars who are not teachers may be in worse straits. Even a nine-to-five job leaves little leisure. Many jobs are more demanding, and most of those likely to be held by

Ph.D.'s or former Ph.D. candidates will provide little or no opportunity for scholarly research. If nonacademic scholars are to carry on research or write, they therefore have even more need for free time than do professors. Though their incomes may be higher and may more closely track increases in the cost of living, their research expenses will be heavier. Unlike professors, they cannot claim such expenses to be job-related and therefore tax-deductible. It is foreseeable that professors and other scholars will be gathered around a trough not adequate for either but with the professors closer.

Here, the power to do something lies with foundations, including the National Endowment for the Humanities. As university resources are shifted to other uses, foundation support of humanists' research and publication will grow in importance. Though not without biases and obligations of their own, foundation trustees and officers are freer than university administrators to deal evenhandedly with academics and nonacademics.

The choices before foundations, however, will be hard. They can support the individuals who seem most promising and give them what they need, or they can alternatively spread grants so that larger numbers of people get a little of what they need. When academics are to be supported, funds might go to those best situated to succeed—those in the stronger colleges and universities—or they might go predominantly to people so situated that they probably cannot do scholarship unless given outside support. Grant-givers will face more agonizingly than ever such dilemmas as choosing between an assistant professor at a rural Southern community college, who has time but no access to libraries, and someone in a New York advertising agency who is six blocks from a great library but has no time to go there.

It may be that any foundations so disposed should simply adopt rules of thumb: a certain percentage of grants to scholars from the faculties of elite schools, a certain percentage to those from the faculties of nonelite schools, and a certain percentage for nonacademics. The obvious argument against such a formula is that it may militate against merit. It could result in not funding a project in one category qualitatively superior to ones funded in other categories. The counterargument is that, absent such a formula, awards are likely to go disproportionately to whichever group is best represented on the jury or juries assessing merit. Approaches to this dilemma already differ from foundation to foundation and will probably continue to do so. Practices appropriate to one foundation will probably not be appropriate for any other. Answerable to the Office of Management and Budget as well as to Congress, the Humanities Endowment must have rules peculiarly its own.

Concerned, as we are, more with the quality than with the sheer quantity of scholarship, we would not urge any foundations or agencies to support nonacademics simply because they are nonacademics. We do, however, venture one suggestion. It is that some foundation or coalition of foundations— probably not including any public agency—consider the possibility of offering a large number of substantial prizes as rewards for completed scholarly work. The first governing principle should be that the prizes be large enough to make meaningful contributions to an individual's income: say, the equivalent of the price of an automobile. The second principle should be that there be enough such prizes so that any serious competitor could regard himself or herself as having a chance of winning.

If the field were limited to articles in major scholarly journals, only 1000 articles or so would have to be considered, for there are not more than 50 major journals in the United States for English, modern languages, history, and philosophy, and few print more than 5 serious articles per issue. One hundred prizes would represent one prize for every 10 articles.

Of course, the institution of prizes could not work miracles. As has recurred in Pulitzer and National Book Award and other prize juries, panels would divide, bicker, and provide public controversy. Even so, the benefits could be greater than the costs.

To begin with, the unit outlay would be relatively small. A prize of $7500 would be only half of the $15,000 that (in 1980 dollars) is a not unusual full-year stipend for a research fellow. If there were 100 such prizes, ample remuneration for judges, and small subsidies for the journals, the total cost could still be less than $1 million a year. Unlike fellowship stipends, furthermore, none of the money would be wasted on fruitless projects. The fruit would already be there to be inspected.

In the second place, prizes would supplement, not substitute for, ordinary income. We do not propose that eligibility be limited to people who do not teach. One reason is the belief that prizes would provide incentives for scholarship to people who teach in schools where research and publication are little appreciated and to professors whose tenure and status exempt them from publish-or-perish pressures. Obviously, rules might exclude people who had recently had sabbaticals or research fellowships. In general, however, we would suggest that competition be as open as possible.

Even so, we would advance as the third and chief argument for the scheme the proposition that it would encourage continued scholarly work by people who possess the training but are not in traditional career paths. The prospect of a substantial prize could provide the necessary extra incentive for night and weekend labor and help to justify it in the eyes of office-mates or superiors with different hobbies. The fact that such rewards would be accessible to people with the requisite training could even affect at the margin decisions by undergraduates on whether or not to seek graduate training.

To sum up: The central question is whether the humanities can retain their vitality during what promises to be a long-swing depression in higher education. It is difficult to project more than 15,000 full-time career openings for college or university teachers in English, modern languages, history, and philosophy from 1980 to the mid-1990s. The number might be even smaller, and not more than half would be at schools offering conditions advantageous for scholarship. If revenues replace enrollments as the controlling factor, numbers of jobs could be greater, but all or almost all scholars would feel increasing strain as a result of dwindling income. There will in all likelihood be many more than 15,000 men and women with doctoral training in the humanities who, by necessity or by choice, will not spend their lives in academic settings. In these circumstances, how is the nation to continue to have a corps of well-qualified, well-trained scholars conserving and adding to learning in the humanities?

Taken all together, the evidence plainly argues that graduate training in the humanities has no necessary connection with a career in college teaching. Though most graduate students aspire to be professors, comparatively few are excited by—or have even thought much about—the prospect of year-in, year-out work in classrooms. Many who do teach find that they do not like it. In any case, they regard graduate work as having done little to improve their ability to teach. They—and Ph.D.'s who do not teach—see the training as having emphasized research skills that have only marginal application in the teaching career itself.

Survey and interview data show graduate students in the humanities to be a varied group, including many combinations of talents and many different personality types. They are suited for a wide variety of other careers.

Humanities Ph.D.'s who have entered business or become government officials have been comparatively satisfied. On the whole, they have found more challenge and variety in their occupations than college professors have found in theirs. They earn more than the professors, and the difference in earnings more than compensates for the fact that what they do makes only indirect use of their doctoral training. On the whole, they also believe that their training makes them better able to think critically and do their jobs. Few regret the time spent on the

Ph.D. A surprisingly large minority have some record of schol-arly accomplishment—a book or an article. They are just about as productive as professors in 4-year colleges, and more pro-ductive than those in 2-year colleges.

At one time it was commonly assumed that, except for dil-ettantes, no one took an undergraduate degree unless headed for a career in teaching or one of the learned professions. Despite ample evidence that liberal arts majors can successfully enter almost any line of work, it is still common for college students to think of those majors in terms of jobs. In reality, any ambitious person is almost certainly better off with an English or history major than with an undergraduate major in business, which in most cases leads only to a career as a clerk or bookkeeper.

The arguments for the usefulness of liberal education for undergraduates cannot be extended wholesale into a case for graduate education. It is not clear just how much value is added to the English or history B.A. by an extra year and certainly not clear how much is added by an extra 7–9 years. Moreover, graduate and undergraduate programs are different in that graduate programs emphasize training over education. They produce scholars.

Our contention is simply that the numbers of people who equip themselves to be scholars should not be a function of actual or anticipated fluctuations in the academic job market. Tens of thousands of young people have the requisite love of subject. The national capacity to provide them with graduate training exists. It will not be a waste if large numbers continue to earn doctorates and go on to posts in insurance companies or government agencies. In fact, the cultural life of the United States will be significantly richer if the training of scholars can be divorced from the preparation of teachers and if it becomes no more extraordinary for a corporate vice-president to have a Ph.D. in philosophy than a law degree and no more re-markable for someone in business or civil service to publish a scholarly book or article than to win an amateur golf tournament or be elected to local office. The humanities could become more integral to American life. If so, "the academic job crisis" would prove to have been a blessing very well disguised.

Appendix

Table A.1

Multiple Regression Analysis of Graduate Students' Propensity for Taking Out Loans to Pay for Graduate School[a,b]

Variable	Simple correlation	Beta when entered	Beta in final step
Selectivity of institution	.16	.155*	.110*
Serious consideration given job in business when student entered graduate school	.12	.130*	.114*
Attractive employment: training officer in business, government	−.10	−.101*	−.074
Personal job prospects in academe compared with graduate students in same field at other schools	.13	.093*	.152*
Personal job prospects in academe compared with graduate students in own department	−.06	−.114*	−.124*
If considering graduate school today, would change institution, not field	.05	.104*	.125*
Method for financing graduate school: own earnings (academic job)	−.18	−.129*	−.263*

(continued)

Appendix

Table A.1
(*continued*)

Variable	Simple correlation	Beta when entered	Beta in final step
Method for financing graduate school: spouse's earnings	−.06	−.118*	−.191*
Method for financing graduate school: university fellowship or scholarship	−.03	−.152*	−.190*
Serious consideration given another discipline when student entered graduate school	−.09	−.084*	−.086*
Method for financing graduate school: foundation or government fellowship	−.03	−.119*	−.121*
Important motivator for pursuing degree: desire to lead more independent work life	.06	.083*	.083*
N			530
R^2			.15

[a] The dependent variable has six codes ranging from (1) none to (6) 81–100%.
[b] $F = 7.65617^*$; $df = 12,517$.
* $p \leq .05$.

Table A.2

Multiple Regression Analysis of Graduate Students' Propensity to Use Own Savings or Other Assets to Pay for Graduate School[a,b]

Variable	Simple correlation	Beta when entered	Beta in final step
Serious consideration given administrative work in college or university when student entered	.13	.132*	.156*
Level of graduate study	− .12	− .124*	− .060
Selectivity of institution	.12	.145*	.114*
Education interrupted since B.A.	.09	.109*	.041
Mother's education	.09	.097*	.052
Attractive employment: college or university administration	− .05	− .093*	− .074
Method for financing graduate school: own earnings (academic job)	− .23*	− .170*	− .462*
Method for financing graduate school: spouse's earnings	− .10	− .164*	− .335*
Method for financing graduate school: university fellowship or scholarship	− .03	− .156*	− .227*
Method for financing graduate school: foundation or government fellowship	− .06	− .179*	− .235*
Method for financing graduate school: own earnings (nonacademic job)	− .03	− .233*	− .235*
Spouse's education	.02	.078*	− .078*
N			530
R^2			.22

[a] The dependent variable has six codes ranging from (1) none to (6) 81–100%.
[b] $F = 12.52016$*; $df = 12,517$.
* $p \leq .05$.

Table A.3

Multiple Regression Analysis of Graduate Students' Propensity to Take Out Loans and Use Own Savings or Other Assets to Finance Graduate School

Variable	Simple correlation	Beta when entered	Beta in final step
Selectivity of institution	.18	.181*	.173*
Level of graduate study	−.13	−.160*	−.044*
Serious consideration given job in business when student entered	.12	.110*	.100*
Mother's education	.10	.106*	.052
Education interrupted since B.A.	.07	.096*	−.007
Serious consideration given administrative work in college or university when student entered	.08	.085*	.094*
Attractive employment: college or university administration	−.08	−.116*	−.086*
Method for financing graduate school: own earnings (academic job)	−.28*	−.202*	−.562*
Method for financing graduate school: spouse's earnings	−.11	−.194*	−.420*
Method for financing graduate school: university fellowship or scholarship	−.04	−.202*	−.364*
Spouse's education	.03	.091*	.115*
If considering graduate school today, would change institution, not field	.02	.082*	.084*
Serious consideration given another discipline when student entered graduate school	−.09	−.082*	−.074*
Method for financing graduate school: foundation or government fellowship	−.06	−.216*	−.281*
Method for financing graduate school: own earnings (nonacademic job)	−.00	−.231*	−.249*

(continued)

Table A.3
(*continued*)

Variable	Simple correlation	Beta when entered	Beta in final step
Personal job prospects compared with other students in own department	− .08	− .078*	− .109*
Overall personal job prospects compared with other students in same field	.11	.090*	.090*
Method for financing graduate school: family contribution	.10	− .082*	− .082*
N			530
R^2			.33

[a] $F = 13.91067$*; $df = 18,511$.
* $p \leq .05$.

Table A.4
Multiple Regression Analysis of Graduate Alumni's Job Satisfaction

Variable	Simple correlation		Beta when entered		Final beta	
	Academic	Nonacademic	Academic	Nonacademic	Academic	Nonacademic
Age	.172	.160	.170*	.148*	.021	.005
Sex	−.079	−.094	−.074*	−.071	.032	.030
Parental income	.088	.039	.103*	.049	.088*	.027
Graduate school selectivity	.076	.004	.064*	−.045	.042	.057
Number of scholarly publications	.201*	.169	.102*	.093	.029	.072
Number of nonscholarly publications	.154	.107	.047	.012	.072*	.020
Expected earnings	.284*	.301*	.098*	.264*	.106*	.264*
Relation of job to field of study	.249*	−.029	.247*	.000	.247*	.017
Part-time employment	−.223*	−.002	−.183*	−.016	−.124*	−.003
N	1046	463				
R^2	.18	.18				
F	9.44646	5.07714				
df	23,1,022	19, 443				

* $p \leq .05$.

Index

Index